Love Them More Than Your Demons

A Christian Man's Guide To Healing Using Scripture

By

William "King" Hollis

© Copyright 2025

All rights reserved. Disclaimer:

This book is published for inspirational and educational purposes only. The reflections, stories, and Scripture passages are intended to encourage healing, faith, and spiritual growth especially for those navigating inner battles, brokenness, and the journey toward restoration.

While biblical truths are presented with care, this book is not a substitute for professional counseling, therapy, medical care, or pastoral guidance. If you are experiencing mental-health challenges, trauma, or significant emotional pain, please seek help from a qualified professional or trusted spiritual advisor.

Scripture Sources & Permissions

Scripture quotations appear in three translations, used with gratitude and in accordance with their respective guidelines:

King James Version (KJV) – Public-domain text; no permission required.

New International Version (NIV)

"Scripture quotations taken from the Holy Bible, New International Version®, NIV®. Copyright © 1973, 1978,

1984, 2011 by Biblica, Inc.® Used by permission. All rights reserved worldwide."

(Fewer than 500 verses quoted and less than 25 % of the total content; no additional permission required.)

New Living Translation (NLT)

"Scripture quotations are taken from the Holy Bible, New Living Translation, copyright © 1996, 2004, 2015 by Tyndale House Foundation. Used by permission of Tyndale House Publishers, Carol Stream, Illinois 60188. All rights reserved."

(Fewer than 500 verses quoted and less than 25 % of the total content; no additional permission required.)

Privacy & Accuracy

Unless explicitly stated, personal stories or identifying details have been shared with permission or have been fictionalized to protect privacy. Any resemblance to real individuals or events is coincidental unless expressly indicated.

All reasonable efforts have been made to ensure accuracy. Nevertheless, the author and publisher assume no liability for how readers use or choose to disregard the material herein.

Copyright

No part of this book may be reproduced, stored in a retrieval system, or transmitted in any form or by any means electronic, mechanical, photocopying, recording, or otherwise without prior written permission from the publisher, except for brief quotations used in reviews, articles, or educational contexts under fair-use provisions.

Special Thanks

First and foremost, I want to thank my wife, Sherita Hollis. She married me as a Muslim while she was a Christian, and through her love, patience, and unwavering faith, she helped lead me to the Lord.

To my pastor, Pastor Rutley thank you for your spiritual guidance and for always standing firm in truth.

To my grandmother, Pamela Burch, and my grandfather, William Hollis you are the roots of my strength and legacy.

To my father, William Hollis Sr., and my mother, Shalawnda Jones thank you for your sacrifices, your love, and the foundation you gave me.

Each of you played a role in shaping the man I am today.

Love Them More Than Your Demons

TABLE OF CONTENTS

FORWARD x

INTRODUCTION xii

CHAPTER 1: The Battle Within......................................1

"For the good that I would I do not: but the evil which I would not, that I do." 1
– Romans 7:19 1
Introduction to the Human Struggle 1
The Strategy for Victory 6
The Hope of Redemption 7
Closing Declaration 17
Prayer.. 19
Journaling Prompts 20

CHAPTER 2: Grace for the Wounded Warrior..........21

"My grace is sufficient for thee: for my strength is made perfect in weakness." 21
– 2 Corinthians 12:9" 21
Introduction to Fear of Being Seen as Weak 21
What Grace Actually Means: The Hope of Redemption 37
Closing Reflection 46
Prayer.. 47
Journaling Prompts 49

CHAPTER 3: Loving Through The Storm 50

"Above all, love each other deeply, because love covers over a multitude of sins." 50

- 1 Peter 4:8 50
Introduction: Loving When It's Not Easy 50
What the Storm Reveals 51
Why Love Is So Powerful 57
Love Like Jesus, Not Like the World 62
Closing Reflection 64
Prayer 67
Journaling Prompts 68

CHAPTER 4: Confronting The Inner Critic 69

"There is therefore now no condemnation to them which are in Christ Jesus." 69
- Romans 8:1 69
Introduction: You Ever Wondered If Grace Was Really For You? 69
How Do You Know This Scripture Is for You? 71
The Truth About Grace 76
Closing Declaration 81
Prayer 82
Journaling Prompts 84

CHAPTER 5: Healing the Father Wound 85

"A father to the fatherless, a defender of widows, is God in his holy dwelling." 85
- Psalm 68:5 85
Introduction: Who Fills the Gap When a Father Isn't There? 85
Why This Scripture Is Critical for Healing 87
The Father You Never Had 90
Closing Reflection 99
Prayer 100
Journaling Prompts 101

CHAPTER 6: Forgiveness as a Weapon 102

"Be kind and compassionate to one another, forgiving each other, just as in Christ God forgave you." 102

– Ephesians 4:32 102

Introduction: Reading Heals the Mind Applying Heals the Heart 102

What Happens When You Don't Forgive 106

The Process of Forgiveness 115

The Power of Applied Scripture 116

Closing Reflection 117

Prayer 119

Reflection Questions 120

CHAPTER 7: The Power of Surrender 121

"Trust in the Lord with all your heart and lean not on your own understanding." 121

– Proverbs 3:5 121

Introduction: You Can't Heal and Control Everything 121

Why This Scripture Is a Lifeline, Not Just a Command 123

Trust Isn't Weak It's Spiritual Strength 125

Why You Can't Lean on Your Own Understanding 127

The Trap of Overthinking 129

When You Trust God, You Rest Differently 134

The Freedom of Surrender 135

Closing Declaration 136

Prayer 138

Reflection Questions 139

CHAPTER 8: Walking Through the Fire 140

"When you walk through the fire, you shall not be burned, nor shall the flame scorch you." 140

– Isaiah 43:2 140

Introduction: The Fire Is Real, But So Is the Promise 140

What the Fire Teaches You 143

What Does It Look Like to Walk Through Fire Without Being Burned? 148

The Purpose of Fire 152

Closing Declaration 155

Prayer 156

Reflection Questions 157

CHAPTER 9: You Can't Heal Alone 158

"As iron sharpens iron, so one person sharpens another." 158

– Proverbs 27:17 158

Introduction: You Need Real Brothers 158

What "Iron Sharpens Iron" Really Means 161

The Cost of Isolation 167

Don't Mistake Loneliness for Strength 168

Closing Declaration 175

Prayer 177

Reflection Questions 178

CHAPTER 10: Becoming Whole Again 179

"He heals the brokenhearted and binds up their wounds." 179

– Psalm 147:3 179

Introduction: What Happens When You Pretend You're Not Bleeding? 179

Let God Be the Surgeon, Not Just the Savior 184

The Hidden Cost of Hidden Wounds 187

Healing Requires Honesty 188

Closing Declaration 195

Prayer 197

Reflection Questions 198

CHAPTER 11: Let Love Kill the Fear 199

"There is no fear in love. But perfect love drives out fear." 199

– 1 John 4:18 199

Introduction: Fear Will Talk You Out of What Love Was Trying to Give You ... 199

Why Fear Has Been Lying to You 201

What is "Perfect Love" 203

The Battle Between Love and Fear 209

Closing Declaration 215

Prayer 217

Reflection Questions 218

Conclusion: Love Them More Than Your Demons ...219

What It Means to Love More Than Your Demons 220

The Power of Supernatural Love 222

Love Like God Loves 223

The Ripple Effect 226

Final Prayer 230

About the Author 232

FORWARD

Every now and then there is someone in our history that achieves greatness even when the odds may seem against them. They rise above the criticism and all the people that seemed to have given up on the possibility of their success.

When they rise, they accomplish things that nobody ever thought were possible. That is exactly what William Hollis has done in a very short period of time and at a young age. If you look at statistics, William wasn't supposed to make it. Having a father in prison and a loving mother who

Unfortunately, he battled with drugs, the world constantly told him that he would never make it out of his environment. He knew he was meant for more and didn't allow anything or anyone to stop him from believing that.

William is someone who truly tapped into his greatest gift which is his ability to transform and inspire people with just the sound of his voice. He spoke himself out of homelessness and is now one of the upcoming top speakers of his generation.

I marvel at his drive, his perseverance, and his desire to make a difference in the lives of so many others. His presence on the stage commands your attention from America to many countries around the world.

Learn all that you can from this book and know that you too can live your dreams. Your circumstances do not predict your story and you have the power to change your direction at any time.

William Hollis is truly an example of exactly what happens when you believe in yourself, embrace your gifts, and you never quit. I call him a son because in many ways he reminds me of my younger self. Passionate, full of life, and always prepared to help his fellow man.

I call him a friend because of his love, generosity and kindness.

May William and the pages of this book bring you the prosperity, motivation, and the true belief that absolutely anything is possible in your life.

Les Brown

INTRODUCTION

There's a silent war raging inside many men, a battle not fought with fists or bullets, but with memories, shame, trauma, pride, and silence. In the name of strength, we've often been taught to suppress our emotions, to "man up" and push through. But unresolved pain doesn't disappear, it only grows louder. It seeps into our relationships, our faith, and our ability to love others.

This book isn't about perfection. It's about progress. It's a call to every man carrying invisible burdens, to every man who loves deeply but struggles to express it. It's for the fathers, husbands, sons, and brothers who need a way back to themselves, and back to God.

Through Scripture, reflection, and raw truth, this book offers a path to healing that begins with one powerful choice: to love deeper than your demons.

Look, I won't sugarcoat this. I've been where you are. I've sat in that dark room at 3 AM, wrestling with thoughts that felt bigger than my faith. I've felt the weight of generational pain pressing on my chest like a hundred-pound stone. I know what it's like to love your family and still feel disconnected from them. To want to be the man God called you to be, yet feel like you're battling yourself every single day.

See, the enemy doesn't just want to destroy you, he wants to use your pain to destroy everyone you love. He wants your unhealed trauma to become your children's inheritance. He wants your silence to become their confusion. He wants your emotional distance to teach them that love comes with walls.

But here's what I learned the hard way: Your demons aren't stronger than your purpose. Your past isn't more powerful than your potential. And the love within you, that God-given ability to heal, protect, provide, and lead, is greater than every lie you've ever been told about yourself.

This isn't just another self-help book. This is a battle plan. It's for the man who's tired of letting pain call the shots. It's for the brother who's ready to break cycles instead of repeat them. It's for the father who wants his children to experience a love that heals, not one that hurts.

Every page you turn is a step toward freedom. Every truth you confront is a wall that comes down. Every time you choose love over fear, healing over hiding, vulnerability over violence, that's when you start winning the war that's been raging inside you.

Your family needs you whole. Your community needs you healed. Your purpose needs you free. And God? He's been waiting for you to see that the very pain you've been running from might be the key to unlocking the man He's always called you to be.

The question isn't whether you're strong enough to face your demons.

The question is: Are you brave enough to love bigger than they are? Let's find out together, in this book.

Why This Book Had to Be Written, I lost my mother. Then, just eleven days before my son was born, I lost my father. And man, it broke me, right at a time in my life when I thought I had it all figured out.

When you start to pray, when you begin to connect with God, you begin to realize something that changes everything: you're bleeding on people.

You're fighting a demon, but you're giving more energy to the demon than to loving your family. You're allowing that demon to spill into the lives of the people closest to you. And that's when I realized, this book had to be written.

This book is a guide to help kings defeat and slay the demons within so they can protect what truly matters, their families, their wives, their children, their mothers, their fathers. It's about unlocking freedom. The freedom to live fully without blaming others or letting anger push away the very people we love.

I believe most men suffer in silence. Because when we do open up, when we share our deepest, most painful truths, it's often turned into a weapon used against us. So we hold it in. We try to deal with it ourselves. But what we don't realize is that over time, it builds up, until we break. And sometimes, we end up doing something, God forbid, terrible to someone we love.

A lot of men show anger toward the women in their lives, but that anger often comes from something deeper. Most men are angriest when they feel they can't provide, when they don't feel like men. It's like a wounded boy trapped inside, not yet grown into what God intended him to be.

I know what I battled. I know what I went through. And I didn't want to keep the way I healed to myself. The way I overcame, transformed, and was able to do great things in my career, that breakthrough wasn't just meant for me. It was meant for you too.

This isn't just another book that borrows from a philosopher in hopes that it works. This is applied knowledge from God. Think of it like a minister breaking down a sermon, he unpacks scripture every time he speaks and puts it into plain language for people to understand.

My goal is to give you a blueprint to recognize who truly holds the keys and who's really in control. A lot of people think they can handle life on their own, but without the Creator leading by example, it's like fighting with your hands tied behind your back.

I don't often use the word religion because, in the Bible, it wasn't emphasized much. The focus was on relationship, our Creator leading by example. People created other religions because they disagreed with certain aspects of Christianity, Islam, or others. But this book can support any man of any faith through the foundation of scripture written in these pages.

Love Them More Than Your Demons

This message comes from a young man like me, someone who has navigated his industry without a manager, without a PR team, just God. I believe that gives me the credibility to offer something people will not only read but actually listen to. And when the audiobook drops, it's going to be even more powerful, because it'll be me speaking directly to you.

This is a gift. A guide to self-rebirth. As you go through these pages and apply the knowledge, you'll begin to transform, and what God does in your life will be nothing short of extraordinary.

The Truth About Your Battle

Here's what I want you to understand before we go any deeper:

- Your anger isn't really about what happened today.
- Your frustration with your woman isn't truly about the dishes, the attitude, or whatever you two are arguing about this week.
- Your distance from your kids isn't just because you're tired from work.

It's about the war inside you that no one talks about. It's about the little boy in you who got hurt and never learned how to heal.

It's about the man you're trying to become fighting against the patterns you inherited.

Most men are walking around with wounds they can't even name.

We're carrying our fathers' pain, our grandfathers' trauma, generations of men who were taught that strength meant silence and love meant control.

But strength without healing is just destruction waiting to happen. Love without wholeness is just pain passing itself down.

You know what changed everything for me? Realizing I wasn't just fighting for myself anymore.

I was fighting for my son's future, for my bloodline, for every man who would come after me.

I was fighting so that the pain would stop with me, and the healing could start with me.

That's what this book is about. It's not just about you getting better, it's about becoming the man who breaks the cycle.

It's about becoming the man who loves so powerfully that it heals both backward and forward.

It's about becoming the man who chooses love over demons, every single time.

Every man reading this has a choice to make:

- You can keep letting your pain drive the car, or you can take back the wheel.
- You can keep bleeding on people, or you can start to heal.
- You can keep running from your demons, or you can learn to love bigger than they are.

This book is your roadmap. Every chapter is a step toward freedom. Every scripture is a weapon against the lies. Every truth I share is a key to unlock the man God always intended you to be.

But here's the thing, I can't do the work for you. I can give you the blueprint, but you've got to build the house. I can show you the path, but you've got to walk it. I can tell you the truth, but you've got to apply it.

The question remains: Are you brave enough to love bigger than your demons?

Turn the page, and let's find out together.

Love Them More Than Your Demons

xx

CHAPTER 1: The Battle Within

"For the good that I would I do not: but the evil which I would not, that I do."

– Romans 7:19

Introduction to the Human Struggle

Look, I need to start this chapter by breaking down something that might shake you to your core. In a single sentence, the Apostle Paul exposes the painful reality every man faces when he tries to live right, and fails. He admits something most men are too ashamed to say out loud: The man I want to be, I keep falling short of. And the man I don't want to be, that's who I keep becoming. This isn't weakness. This is war. A war between two natures.

Every man walks with two sides: the spirit and the flesh. The spirit craves peace, purpose, and power through God. But the flesh chases impulse, ego, and escape. Paul is telling us that even he, a chosen apostle, wasn't immune to this internal tension. He had the desire to do good, to live righteously, to walk in God's will, yet he often found himself doing the opposite. This isn't just sin, it's conflict. And understanding that conflict is the first step toward healing.

Let's be real. How many times have you said, "I'm done with this. I won't go back. This time is different",only to end up in the same room, the same trap, the same habits? That doesn't make you a bad man. It means healing requires more than good intentions. It takes spiritual power, radical honesty, and discipline.

What Paul is describing is the frustration every man feels when he fails his own standards. It's the pull of addiction, lust, pride, violence, laziness, even depression. It's doing what you hate because it feels familiar, even when it's slowly killing you.

But here's the truth every man needs to understand, the difference between shame and conviction:

Shame says you'll never change. Conviction says you can change, but you need help. And that's where God steps in.

This verse makes one thing clear: struggling doesn't mean you're fake. It means you're human. You're not disqualified. You're in process.

See, the problem isn't that you're broken. The problem is that you've been fighting a spiritual war with natural weapons. You've been trying to overcome supernatural opposition using willpower alone. That's like bringing a water gun to a battlefield.

Paul understood something most men miss: you don't win the war by trying harder, you win it by surrendering to the right Commander.

Many men are fighting daily, yet they don't know the enemy, the battleground, or the stakes. So they bleed in silence, assuming it's just bad luck, bad habits, or "just the way I've always been." But Paul, in Romans 7:19, exposes the truth: this isn't coincidence, it's combat. And you can't win a war you don't even know you're in. That's the first thing you need to understand about the battle within.

I want you to start paying attention to the patterns in your life. Do you keep making promises to yourself that you don't keep? Do you feel like two different men, the one in your heart and the one in your habits? Do you ever wake up wondering, "Why do I feel so empty, even when good things surround me?"

When a man sees his own repeated struggles, that's not failure, that's a fight. And the moment you recognize it, you can begin to change it.

Pay Attention to the Patterns

Ask yourself these questions:
- Do you keep making promises to yourself that you never follow through on?
- Do you feel like you're living as two different men, the one in your heart and the one in your habits?
- Do you ever wake up wondering, "Why do I feel so empty, even when everything around me seems good?"

Recognizing your repeated struggles isn't failure, it's a sign you're still in the fight. And the moment you see it clearly, you can begin to change it.

Recognize the Signs of Spiritual Warfare

Men often think spiritual warfare looks like demons or exorcisms, but in reality, it looks like this: sudden mood swings toward self-hate, constant distractions when you try to pray or read, a strong pull back into destructive habits right after a breakthrough, and isolating yourself when you most need support. That's not random, that's targeted.

You're not just moody, you're under spiritual pressure. Understanding this shifts the perspective from personal failure to spiritual warfare.

If the voice in your head sounds more like condemnation than conviction, more like shame than correction, that's not God speaking. That's the enemy. If you believe you're just lazy, broken, or beyond help, that belief is already part of the battle. God doesn't just expose sin, He invites healing.

Some men don't know how to articulate what they're going through. They just say, "I feel lost. I'm tired of myself. I keep messing up." What they're describing is a spiritual war, a battle between the man they're called to be and the forces that keep pulling them back. It's not just behavior, it's warfare. And you don't have to stay trapped in it.

Once a man realizes the battle is spiritual, he stops relying on willpower alone and starts depending on God's power. Many men turn their anger inward, blaming themselves, their past, or even God. But Scripture reminds us: "We wrestle not against flesh and blood, but against spiritual wickedness" (Ephesians 6:12). The real enemy isn't you, it's the Enemy lying to you, tempting you, and whispering that you'll never be more than your mistakes. You need to redirect the fight outward and step into battle with God at your side.

Here's what you need to do:

Identify your patterns. What is the evil you struggle with? Is it anger, addiction, lust, dishonesty, or selfishness? Name it. Don't hide from the battle, hiding only gives it more power.

Pray over it. Bring it into the light. The enemy thrives in darkness but withers in the presence of truth and prayer.

Invite accountability. Healing doesn't happen in isolation. Every king needs wise counsel and trusted battle brothers. Find men who will fight with you, not judge you.

Renew your mind. Romans 12:2 says, "Be transformed by the renewing of your mind." You can't fight spiritual battles with worldly weapons. Fill your mind with God's truth, not the world's lies.

The Strategy for Victory

Here's what you need to do:

Identify your patterns. What is the evil you wrestle with? Is it anger, addiction, lust, dishonesty, or selfishness?

Name it. Don't run from the struggle, hiding it only gives it more power.

Pray over it. Bring it into the light. The enemy thrives in darkness but withers in the presence of truth and prayer.

Invite accountability. Healing doesn't happen in isolation. Every king needs wise counsel and trusted battle brothers. Surround yourself with men who will fight alongside you, not judge you.

Paul's cry in Romans 7 carries over into Romans 8, and that's where hope begins to rise. He declares, "There is therefore now no condemnation for those who are in Christ Jesus" (Romans 8:1). Your struggle doesn't make you a failure; it reveals your deep need for a Savior. It's not about achieving perfection, it's about being willing to keep fighting. And even when you stumble, you fall into the arms of mercy, not judgment.

The Hope of Redemption

Brother, what you're experiencing isn't unique to you. Every man who has ever tried to live righteously has felt this tension. The difference between men who overcome and those who stay stuck isn't the absence of struggle, it's the willingness to name the struggle and fight it with God's power rather than their own.

You're not crazy for feeling like you're fighting yourself. You're not weak for admitting you need help. You're not disqualified because you've failed before. You're human, and humans were created to need their Creator.

The enemy wants you to believe you're the only one fighting this fight. He wants you to think you're too far gone, too broken, too damaged. But that's a lie from the pit of hell. The very fact that you feel convicted about your sin means the Holy Spirit is still working in you. The very fact that you hate what you do means your heart isn't completely hardened. That internal conflict Paul describes isn't evidence of failure, it's evidence of God's grace still pursuing you.

I know what it's like to feel split in two. I know what it's like to love God and want to do right, yet find yourself in situations you swore you'd never be in again. I know what it's like to look in the mirror and not recognize the man staring back.

That war inside you, the one that feels like it's going to tear you apart? That's not a sign you're beyond hope.

That's a sign you're not dead yet. It's a sign there's still something in you worth fighting for.

I've been in that place, angry at yourself for being angry, disappointed in yourself for being disappointed, hating yourself for hating. That's the cycle Paul talks about in Romans 7:19. It's not just about sin, it's about the frustration that comes from knowing better but not always doing better. It's about having a heart that longs to honor God but flesh that keeps pulling you in the opposite direction.

And here's what the enemy wants you to believe: that this internal conflict means you're not truly saved, not really changed, not actually a man of God. He wants you to think that real Christians don't struggle like this. He wants you to believe that if you were genuinely walking with God, you wouldn't have these thoughts, these temptations, these moments of weakness. But that's a lie straight from hell.

The very fact that you're conflicted about your sin is proof that God's Spirit is alive in you. The very fact that you feel convicted when you do wrong is evidence that you haven't been handed over to a reprobate mind. The very fact that you want to change, even when change feels impossible, means there's still hope for you. Dead men don't feel guilty. Dead men don't wrestle with conviction. Dead men don't hate their sin.

Let me tell you something that might shock you: God isn't surprised by your struggle. He's not in heaven disappointed that you're not perfect yet. He's not checking His watch wondering when you'll finally get your act together. He knew exactly what He was getting when He saved you. He saw every failure, every relapse, every moment of weakness you'd ever have, and He chose you anyway.

But here's where most men get it twisted: they think that because God isn't surprised by their struggle, they can just keep struggling without fighting. They assume grace means they can remain comfortable in their sin. But that's not what Paul is teaching in Romans 7. Paul isn't giving us permission to stay stuck, he's giving us clarity about why we feel stuck, so we can break free.

The difference between a man who stays in bondage and a man who walks in freedom isn't the absence of struggle, it's the decision to stop fighting the battle alone. It's the willingness to admit that willpower isn't enough, that good intentions aren't sufficient, that trying harder isn't the answer. The answer is complete dependence on God's power working through you.

When I lost my mother, and then my father, just 11 days before my son was born, I found myself in a place where I was bleeding on everyone around me. I was giving more energy to my demons than to loving my family. I was fighting a war inside my heart, but I let that war spill over onto the people I loved most.

That's what unresolved trauma does. It doesn't just hurt you, it hurts everyone in your path.

But here's what I learned during that season of my life:

- You can't heal what you won't acknowledge.
- You can't overcome what you won't name.
- You can't defeat what you pretend doesn't exist.

The first step to victory isn't pretending you're not struggling, it's admitting that you are and that you need help.

Most men think asking for help makes them weak. But I'm here to tell you: pretending you don't need help when you do, that's what makes you weak.

Real strength isn't the ability to carry every burden on your own.

Real strength is the wisdom to know when to set the burden down, and let someone stronger help you carry it.

And that's exactly what Paul figured out. In Romans 7, he cries out, "O wretched man that I am! Who will deliver me from this body of death?" But he doesn't stop there.

In Romans 8:1, he declares, "There is therefore now no condemnation to those who are in Christ Jesus."

Paul learned that the battle isn't won by trying harder, it's won by trusting deeper.

You see, the enemy has been using the same playbook for thousands of years. He wants you to believe that your struggle disqualifies you. That your failure makes you irredeemable. That your past mistakes define your future.

But God has a different narrative for your life.

God says your struggle doesn't disqualify you, it qualifies you for grace.

Your failure doesn't make you irredeemable, it makes you a candidate for redemption.

Your past doesn't define your future, it becomes the testimony of God's transforming power in your life.

The question isn't whether you'll struggle.

- The question is: What will you do with your struggle?
- Will you let it drive you away from God, or draw you closer to Him?
- Will you let it make you bitter, or make you better?
- Will you let it become your excuse, or your opportunity?

I want you to understand something that changed my life: your lowest moments can become launching pads, if you let God use them. The place where you feel most broken can become the very space where God does His greatest work. The area where you feel most defeated can become the ground where you experience your greatest victory.

But it all starts with honesty. It begins with admitting that you can't save yourself. It starts with acknowledging that you need a Savior, one bigger than your sin, stronger than your flesh, and more faithful than your feelings. It begins with recognizing that the battle isn't just about changing behavior; it's about transforming the heart.

See, most men believe the goal is to reach a place where they never struggle again. That's not reality. The true goal is to learn how to fight the struggle with the right weapons. It's to stop fighting alone and start fighting with the army of heaven at your back. It's realizing that your struggle doesn't disqualify you from God's love, it actually qualifies you for His grace.

Every time you choose to turn to God instead of away from Him in the middle of your struggle, you're winning. Every time you refuse to let shame stop you from praying, you're winning. Every time you choose transparency over hiding, you are winning. Victory isn't about never falling, it's about rising every time you do, and turning your face toward the One who lifts you up.

This inner battle won't vanish anytime soon, but it doesn't have to destroy you. In fact, it can become the very thing that draws you closer to God than you've ever been. When you realize you can't save yourself, you start depending on the One who already did. When you admit you can't fix yourself, you begin surrendering to the One who can transform you from the inside out.

But let me show you what surrender really means, because many men get this wrong too. Surrender isn't giving up; it's giving over. It's not about passivity, it's about partnership with God. It's not about quitting the fight, it's about letting the right Commander lead the charge.

When you surrender to God, you're not waving a white flag of defeat. You're raising a battle banner that says, "I can't do this alone, but I don't have to." You're not admitting weakness; you're accessing strength. You're not acknowledging failure; you're stepping into a position for victory.

And here's what happens when you start fighting with God instead of fighting alone: the battle doesn't necessarily get easier, but you become stronger. The enemy doesn't stop attacking, but you begin winning. The struggle doesn't disappear, but it stops controlling you.

I've learned that the men who overcome aren't those who never struggle, they're the ones who struggle with purpose. They understand that every battle they fight and win strengthens them for the next one. They know that every temptation they resist builds spiritual endurance. They recognize that every time they choose God over their flesh, they're becoming more like the man He called them to be.

But this process isn't quick, and it certainly isn't easy. It requires a level of patience with yourself that most men don't possess. It requires grace for your failures that many men struggle to give themselves. It requires hope for your future, even when it feels out of reach.

The enemy wants you to believe that if you don't change overnight, you'll never change at all. He wants you to think that if you don't see immediate results, God isn't working. He wants you to believe that transformation should be instant, and that if it's not, something's wrong with you.

But God operates on a different timeline than your impatience. He's more interested in lasting change than quick fixes. He's more concerned with heart transformation than surface-level behavior. He's more focused on who you're becoming than what you're doing right now.

That's why Paul could write in Philippians 1:6: "Being confident of this very thing, that He who has begun a good work in you will complete it until the day of Jesus Christ." God doesn't start what He doesn't intend to finish. He doesn't begin a transformation He doesn't plan to complete. He doesn't save you only to leave you stuck.

The work He's doing in you runs deeper than you realize, and it's bigger than you can see. Every struggle you face is an opportunity for Him to display His power. Every weakness you admit is a space for Him to demonstrate His strength. Every failure you experience is a moment for Him to extend His grace.

So when you find yourself doing the very thing you hate, don't let it drive you to despair, let it drive you to dependence. When patterns in your life keep repeating, don't let them convince you that you'll never change, let them remind you that you need God's power to change. And when you feel like you're fighting a losing battle, don't surrender to defeat, surrender to the One who's already won the war.

Closing Declaration

So when you find yourself doing the very thing you hate, don't let it drive you to despair, let it drive you to dependence.

When you notice patterns in your life that keep repeating, don't let them convince you that you'll never change. Let them convince you that you need God's power to change.

When you feel like you're fighting a losing battle, don't surrender to defeat, surrender to the One who's already won the war.

Brother, if you're doing things you hate, you're not alone.

If you're tired of failing, take heart. Even Paul failed, but he didn't stay down.

The fight you're in? It's proof you're alive. Proof you haven't given up.

The goal isn't to avoid struggle forever. The goal is to keep turning toward God, even in the middle of the struggle.

Your demons don't disqualify you from loving yourself or those around you.

They remind you that you need a Savior bigger than your struggles, stronger than your flesh, and more faithful than your failures.

The war is real. But so is the victory waiting for you on the other side.

Prayer

Father, I thank You that even in my struggle,

You see me as Your son. I confess that I've been trying to fight battles. You never intended me to fight alone.

I name my struggles before You now. I bring my patterns, my failures, my shame into

Your light. Give me the courage to stop hiding and start healing.

Remind me that my struggle doesn't disqualify me it qualifies me for Your grace.

Help me to love deeper than my demons and fight harder than my flesh.

In Jesus' name,

Amen.

William "King" Hollis

Journaling Prompts

- What patterns do you see in your life that you've been calling "weakness" that might actually be spiritual warfare?
- Write about a time you felt like "two different men." What was the conflict between who you wanted to be and who you were being?
- What voices in your head sound more like condemnation than conviction? How can you begin to distinguish between God's voice and the enemy's lies?
- If you truly believed this struggle was a war and not a personal failing, how would that change how you approach it?
- What would it look like for you to "surrender to the right commander" in this battle?

CHAPTER 2: Grace for the Wounded Warrior

"My grace is sufficient for thee: for my strength is made perfect in weakness."
– 2 Corinthians 12:9"

Introduction to Fear of Being Seen as Weak

Let's be honest, most men would rather bleed in silence than admit they're hurting. We've been conditioned to believe that strength means silence, that power requires perfection, and that asking for help signals failure. So, we suffer quietly. We snap at the people we love. We hide behind our jobs, our bodies, our hustle, and sometimes even behind our ministry, so no one sees the broken pieces.

But in one powerful scripture, God flips the entire idea of masculinity on its head. He tells us something most men have never heard before: you're strongest when you admit you're weak. That sounds backward, right? But stay with me, because this might be the truth that saves your life.

Remember what Paul wrote in Romans 7:19: "For the good that I would, I do not: but the evil which I would not, that I do." In that verse, Paul exposed the painful reality faced by every man who has ever tried to live right and failed. He admitted something most men are too ashamed to say out loud: The man I want to be, I keep falling short of. And the man I don't want to be, that's who I keep becoming.

This isn't weakness. This is war, the war of two natures.

The War Continues in Our Weakness

Every man walks with two sides, the spirit and the flesh. The spirit seeks peace, purpose, and power through God. But the flesh chases impulse, ego, and escape. Paul understood this internal conflict better than most. That's exactly why God chose him to demonstrate strength through weakness.

This isn't just sin, it's a struggle. And recognizing that struggle is the first step toward healing. What Paul discovered, and what every man needs to grasp, is that our weakness isn't a disqualification. It's an invitation for God's power to step in.

Let's be real. How many times have you said, "I'm done with this," "I won't go back," "This time is different", only to find yourself in the same room, caught in the same trap, repeating the same habits? That's not because you're a bad man. It's because healing takes more than good intentions. It demands spiritual power, brutal honesty, and real discipline.

What Paul is describing is what every man feels after falling short of his own standards. It's the pull of addiction, lust, pride, violence, laziness, even depression. It's doing what you hate simply because it feels familiar, even when it's slowly destroying you.

Paul Had Power and Still Struggled

This verse comes from a letter Paul wrote, where he openly admits he was dealing with something painful, a thorn in his flesh. We don't know exactly what it was, but we know it kept him humble. He asked God three times to take it away. And what did God say? "My grace is sufficient for you. My strength is made perfect in your weakness." In other words, I'm not going to remove the struggle, I'm going to reveal My power through it.

Let that sink in for a moment. Paul, the same man who wrote most of the New Testament, planted churches across the known world, and had supernatural encounters with God, this same man struggled with something that brought him to his knees. And instead of removing it, God used it to demonstrate His power.

That alone should tell you something. If Paul, with all his spiritual authority and divine encounters, still struggled with something that made him feel weak, what makes you think you're supposed to have it all figured out? What makes you think your struggle disqualifies you from being used by God?

Here's the key difference between shame and conviction, something every man needs to understand: Shame says you'll never change. Conviction says you can change, but you need help. And this is exactly where God steps in. This verse makes it clear: just because you're struggling doesn't mean you're fake, it means you're human. You're not disqualified. You're in progress.

Men Hate Feeling Weak Until They Understand It

As men, we hate the feeling of being out of control. We hate needing help. We hate breaking down. But that's pride in disguise, and pride is a silent killer. God never called men to be invincible. He called us to be vessels, carriers of His power. And a vessel that's cracked lets more light shine through.

Your tears don't make you less of a man, they make you human. Your battles don't disqualify you, they make you a candidate for grace. Your breakdown might just be the beginning of your breakthrough.

See, we've been taught that real men don't cry, real men don't ask for help, real men handle everything on their own. But that's not biblical masculinity, that's cultural masculinity. That's the world's definition of strength, not God's. And the world's definition of strength will destroy you if you let it.

I've seen too many men crushed by that lie. I've watched marriages fall apart because a man was too proud to ask for help. I've seen fathers lose their children because they couldn't humble themselves enough to say, "I'm struggling." I've witnessed brothers take their own lives because they believed admitting weakness was worse than ending it all.

But God has a different definition of strength. His strength doesn't erase your weakness, it is perfected through it. His power doesn't hide your struggles, it transforms them into testimonies.

Redefine Strength: A Man at War Needs Strategy
- Strength isn't about pretending.
- Strength is showing up anyway.
- Strength is returning to your children even when you feel like you've failed them.
- Strength is praying when you don't feel worthy.
- Strength is choosing therapy or a men's group over drugs, alcohol, or violence.
- Strength is saying, "God, I can't carry this alone."

God's grace doesn't appear when you're flexing, it appears when you're failing.

You don't win the war by trying harder. You win it by surrendering to the right Commander.

Here's how:

Identify Your Patterns. What is the "evil that I do"? Is it anger, addiction, sexual sin, dishonesty, or selfishness? Name it.

Don't Hide the Struggle. Hiding it makes it stronger. Confess it. Pray over it. Bring it into the light.

Invite Accountability. Healing doesn't happen in isolation. Every king needs wise counsel and a battle brother.

Renew Your Mind. Romans 12:2 says be transformed by the renewing of your mind. You can't fight spiritual battles with worldly weapons.

There's a reason God works through weakness: because when you're strong in your own power, you don't seek Him. It's when you have nothing left that He finally has room to move. And when the world sees a man fall and still rise, they recognize God in it.

When you try to be everything for everyone, you leave no room for God to be your everything. But when you admit you can't do it all, when you acknowledge your need for help, when you surrender the urge to appear strong, that's when God can truly show up and show out in your life.

Every man knows what it's like to carry weight he was never meant to carry alone. Whether it's financial pressure, family responsibilities, or personal struggles, we've all been in that place where we're drowning but still telling everyone we're fine. We pretend to have it all together while quietly falling apart inside. But it's in those breakdown moments, when we finally admit we can't handle it, that God begins to work in ways we never expected.

That breakdown you fear? It might be your breakthrough. That moment of weakness you're ashamed of? It might be the foundation for the strength God wants to build in you.

Let me tell you what I've learned about surrendering to God's strength through our weakness: it's not a one-time decision, it's a daily choice. Every morning, you have to ask yourself again: Am I going to try to be strong in my own power, or will I depend on God's strength working through my weakness?

Most men believe that once they surrender to God, the struggle should become easier. But that's not how it works. The struggle doesn't necessarily get easier, you get stronger.

The challenges don't vanish, you develop the spiritual muscle to overcome them. The weakness doesn't disappear, you learn how to let God's strength flow through it.

You see, the enemy doesn't stop attacking just because you surrendered to God. In fact, he often intensifies his attacks, knowing you're becoming dangerous. When a man learns to access God's strength through his weakness, he becomes a threat to everything the enemy is trying to achieve.

But here's what truly changes when you surrender: You stop fighting alone. You stop trying to win battles in your own strength. You stop pretending you have it all figured out. You start depending on the God who has already won every battle you'll ever face.

This is what Paul understood when he wrote about his thorn in the flesh. He could have spent his life bitter about the struggle God didn't remove. He could have questioned God's love because of the weakness he had to carry. He could have walked away from his calling because he didn't feel strong enough.

But instead, Paul learned to boast in his weakness. He celebrated the very thing that made him feel inadequate, because he discovered that's where God's power showed up most clearly. He realized his weakness wasn't a hindrance to God's plan, it was part of it.

That's a level of maturity many men never reach. Most spend their lives trying to eliminate their weaknesses, rather than learning how to let God use them. Most see their limitations as disqualifications, instead of opportunities for God to reveal His power.

But when you truly understand that God's strength is made perfect in weakness, everything changes. Your struggles become your ministry. Your pain becomes your platform. Your weakness becomes your weapon.

I've seen this truth transform men's lives in ways that once seemed impossible. I've watched men who were addicted to drugs become powerful ministers of restoration. I've seen men who struggled with anger become gentle fathers and loving husbands. I've witnessed men who battled depression become sources of hope for others walking through darkness.

So what made the difference? They stopped running from their weakness and started running with it, straight into the arms of God. They stopped hiding their struggles and began using them to help others. They stopped viewing their pain as a disqualification and started seeing it as their assignment.

But this kind of transformation requires something most men are reluctant to give: time. We live in a microwave culture that craves instant results, but God works through a slow-cooking process that develops deep, lasting change.

The enemy will use your impatience against you. He'll whisper that if you were truly surrendered to God, you would have changed by now. He'll suggest that if God's strength were really working through your weakness, you wouldn't still be struggling. He'll try to convince you that transformation should be immediate, and that if it's not, something must be wrong with you or your faith.

But that's not how spiritual growth works. It's more like physical growth, gradual, sometimes imperceptible, but always occurring when you consistently choose to depend on God's strength instead of your own.

Think about it this way: When you go to the gym, you don't expect massive results after one workout. You understand that building physical strength takes time, consistency, and patience. The same is true of spiritual strength. Every time you choose to trust God in your weakness, you're building spiritual muscle. Every time you choose vulnerability over hiding, you're developing character. Every time you choose dependence on God over self-reliance, you're growing in maturity.

And just like physical growth, spiritual growth unfolds in seasons. There are times of rapid progress and times of apparent stagnation. There are seasons when you feel like you're advancing, and seasons when it seems you're moving backward. But if you continue choosing to rely on God's strength in your weakness, you're always moving forward, even when you can't see it.

A Message to the Brother Who Feels Like He's Failing

If you feel like your life is unraveling, if the weight feels too heavy, if you're tired of pretending to be strong, you're in the perfect place for God's strength to show up.

Don't run from the weakness. Don't hide in the noise. Don't mask it with anger. Sit with it, and bring it to God. Say:

"Lord, I don't feel strong enough to carry this, but I know Your grace is enough for me." That's not giving up. That's giving over.

See, most men think that admitting weakness means they've failed as men. But the opposite is true. Admitting weakness means you're finally ready to become the man God called you to be.

Pretending to be strong when you're not, that's what failure looks like.

Acknowledging your need for God's strength, that's what success looks like.

The enemy wants you to believe that real men handle everything alone. He wants you to think that needing God's help somehow makes you less masculine. But that's a lie designed to keep you isolated, struggling, and ultimately defeated.

God designed you to need Him. He created you to depend on His strength, not to live independently from it.

When you try to be strong in your own power, you're actually working against the very design God intended for your life.

This is where most men get confused about biblical masculinity. They think being a godly man means being self-sufficient, emotionally closed off, and never needing help. But that's not what the Bible teaches.

Look at the men God used throughout Scripture, they were all men who learned to rely on His strength through their weakness.

Moses felt inadequate as a speaker, but God used his weakness to demonstrate divine power through the plagues and the exodus.

David was just a shepherd boy facing a giant, but God used his weakness to show that the battle belongs to the Lord.

Gideon was hiding in a winepress when God called him a mighty warrior, but God used his fear and uncertainty to prove that victory comes through divine strength, not human might.

Peter was impulsive and prone to failure, but God used his weakness to build His Church.

Paul had a thorn in his flesh that kept him humble, but God used that weakness to spread the gospel across the known world.

Even Jesus, in His humanity, cried out on the cross, "My God, my God, why have You forsaken Me?", showing us that even the Son of God experienced moments of weakness and deep anguish.

The pattern is clear: God doesn't choose perfect men. He chooses available men.

He doesn't look for men who have it all figured out. He looks for men who are willing to trust Him when they don't.

He doesn't need you to be strong. He needs you to be surrendered.

Surrendering to God's strength through your weakness isn't a passive act. It's not about giving up and letting life happen to you, it's about actively choosing to trust God's power instead of relying on your own. It means intentionally seeking His wisdom rather than depending on your limited understanding. It's purposefully inviting His strength to work through your weakness instead of trying to conquer it alone.

This calls for a fundamental shift in how you view masculinity. Strength isn't the ability to handle everything on your own; it's the wisdom to know when you need help. Vulnerability isn't weakness; it's courage. Asking for help isn't failure; it's strength.

When you embrace this shift, everything changes. Your relationships deepen because you stop hiding behind a mask. Your faith strengthens because you rely on God instead of yourself. Your impact grows because people are drawn to authenticity, not perfection.

But to live this way, you have to unlearn the lies you've been taught about manhood. You've been conditioned to believe that showing emotion is weakness, but God gave you emotions for a purpose. You've been told that asking for help is failure, but God created community because He knew you weren't meant to do life alone. You've been taught that vulnerability is dangerous, but God calls you into relationships that demand honesty and openness.

These lies have trapped you in cycles of isolation, pride, and defeat. They've convinced you to carry every burden alone, fight every battle solo, and solve every problem without help. But that's not strength, that's stubbornness. That's not masculinity, that's foolishness.

Real strength is having the courage to admit when you're wrong. Real masculinity is having the humility to ask for help. Real power is having the wisdom to depend on God's strength instead of your own.

When you live out this truth, you become the kind of man others want to follow, not because you're perfect, but because you're real. Not because you have all the answers, but because you know where to find them. Not because you're the strongest person in the room, but because you're connected to the strongest God in the universe.

What Grace Actually Means: The Hope of Redemption

Grace doesn't mean you won't struggle. It doesn't mean you won't slip. Grace means that even when you do, you are still loved, still chosen, still powerful.

"My grace is sufficient", that means when you mess up, grace is enough. When you relapse, grace is enough. When you want to quit, grace is enough. When you cry in the dark, grace is enough.

Paul's cry about doing what he hated carries into Romans 8, and that's where the hope lives. He writes, "There is therefore now no condemnation for those who are in Christ Jesus" (Romans 8:1).

The struggle doesn't make you a failure, it reveals your need for a Savior. It's not about being perfect. It's about being willing to fight. And even when you fall, you fall into the arms of mercy, not judgment.

Grace isn't God's Plan B for when you fail. Grace is God's Plan A for how you succeed. It's not a consolation prize for weakness, it's the very power that transforms your weakness into strength.

But here's what most men miss about grace: it's not just forgiveness for your failures. Grace is also the power to overcome them. It's not just God saying, "It's okay that you messed up."

Grace is God saying, "I'm going to give you the strength to overcome what you couldn't conquer on your own."

When Paul asked God three times to remove his thorn, God didn't say, "Just deal with it."

He said, "My grace is sufficient." In other words, "I won't take away your struggle, but I'll give you everything you need to turn that struggle into strength."

That's what grace does. It doesn't eliminate your battles, it equips you to win them. It doesn't remove your challenges, it empowers you to overcome them. It doesn't make you perfect, it makes you powerful.

The Strongest Thing You Can Do

Brother, hear me: You are not less of a man because you're hurting. You are not less of a man because you feel like quitting. You are not less of a man because you need

God every single day. You are not failing, you're finally letting go of the mask. And that's when God says, "Now I can use you."

Let your weakness become your weapon. Let your pain become your pulpit. Let your scars tell a story that brings someone else back to life. Because the moment you surrender your strength is the moment you step into His.

The strongest men I know aren't the ones who never struggle, they're the ones who struggle with purpose. They're the ones who understand that their weakness isn't a disqualification, it's a qualification for God's power. They're the ones who have learned that admitting they need help doesn't make them less of a man, it makes them more of the man God has called them to be.

Your weakness isn't your enemy, it's your invitation. It's God's way of saying, "Stop trying to do this alone. Let Me show you what real strength looks like."

When you stop hiding your struggles and start sharing them, you give other men permission to do the same. When you stop pretending to have it all together and start being honest about your need for God, you become a leader worth following. When you stop trying to be perfect and start being real, you become powerful in ways you never imagined.

The world doesn't need another man pretending to be strong. The world needs more men who are brave enough to be real. The world needs men who understand that true strength comes from God, not from themselves. The world needs men who know that their weakness isn't their downfall, it's their weapon.

See, you've learned something most men never figure out: your greatest breakthrough is often hidden in your biggest breakdown. That place where you feel most vulnerable, most exposed, most ashamed, that's exactly where God wants to meet you. That's where He wants to do His greatest work.

Many men know what it's like to sit in moments of complete weakness, whether it's after losing a loved one, facing a major failure, or dealing with overwhelming pressure. You feel weak. You feel broken. You feel like you're letting down everyone who's counting on you to be strong. But it's in those moments of total surrender that God begins to teach you what true strength really is.

Real strength isn't pretending you're okay when you're not. Real strength isn't putting on a mask for those around you. Real strength is admitting you can't carry it all, and asking God to carry what you can't.

That's when I learned this: God never wastes your pain, He uses it. He never wastes your struggle, He transforms it. He never wastes your weakness, He reveals His strength through it.

But here's what I want you to understand: This process isn't comfortable. It asks you to sit with your pain instead of numbing it. It asks you to face your fears instead of running from them. It asks you to admit your limitations instead of pretending they don't exist.

Most men run from this process because it feels like death. And in a way, it is. It's the death of the false self you've been trying to maintain. The death of the image you've been projecting. The death of the lie that you can handle everything on your own.

But resurrection looks like this: It's discovering you're more powerful when you're honest than when you're hiding. It's realizing you're more influential when you're real than when you're "perfect." It's understanding that people don't need you to have it all together they need you to show them how to trust God when you don't.

The enemy wants you to believe vulnerability is weakness. He wants you to think asking for help is failure. He wants you to believe admitting you're struggling means you're not a real man. But that's backwards thinking that keeps you trapped in cycles of defeat.

God says the opposite. He says vulnerability is courage. Asking for help is wisdom. Admitting you're struggling? That's the beginning of breakthrough.

When you understand this, everything changes. Your struggles become your ministry. Your pain becomes your platform.

Your testimony becomes your weapon against the enemy's lies.

I've seen men transform their entire lives when they finally grasped this truth.

I've watched marriages get restored when a man admitted he needed help.

I've seen fathers reconnect with their children when they stopped pretending to be perfect and started being real.

I've witnessed brothers step into their purpose when they stopped running from their pain and started using it. But transformation doesn't happen overnight.

It requires a kind of patience with yourself that most men lack.

It calls for grace for your failures that many men struggle to give themselves.

It demands hope for a future that some have stopped believing in.

The enemy will tell you that if you don't change immediately, you'll never change at all.

He'll whisper that if you don't see instant results, God isn't working.

He'll try to convince you that transformation should be quick, and that if it's not, something's wrong with you.

But God operates on a different timeline than your impatience.

He's more interested in deep change than in quick fixes. He's more concerned with heart transformation than behavior modification.

He's more focused on who you're becoming than on what you're doing right now.

That's why Paul could confidently say in Philippians 1:6,

"Being confident of this very thing, that He who has begun a good work in you will complete it until the day of Jesus Christ."

God doesn't start what He doesn't plan to finish.

He doesn't begin a transformation He doesn't intend to complete.

He doesn't save you just to leave you stuck.

The work He's doing in you, through your weakness, is deeper than you realize and greater than you can see.

Every moment you choose to trust Him in your weakness builds spiritual muscle.

Every time you choose vulnerability over hiding, you develop character.

Every time you choose dependence on God over self-reliance, you position yourself for greater impact.

Your weakness isn't slowing down God's plan for your life, it's accelerating it.

It's not disqualifying you from your purpose, it's preparing you for it.

It's not making you less effective, it's making you more authentic.

Authenticity is what the world is desperately searching for. People are tired of perfect Instagram posts and carefully curated highlight reels. They're hungry for real men, men who are honest about their struggles while pointing others to the God who gives them strength.

When you embrace your weakness instead of hiding it, you become that man. When you share your struggles instead of pretending they don't exist, you become a voice of hope for others who are silently suffering. When you show people how God's strength works through your weakness, you become a living testimony of His power.

This is why the enemy fights so hard to keep you ashamed of your weakness. He knows your honesty could be the key that unlocks freedom for someone else. He knows your transparency about your need for God could be the testimony that leads another man to surrender.

So when you feel weak, remember that you're in good company. Paul felt weak. David felt weak. Moses felt weak. Peter felt weak. Every man God has ever used in a significant way has felt the weight of his own inadequacy and the desperate need for God's strength.

The difference between men who overcome and men who stay stuck isn't the absence of weakness, it's what they do with their weakness. Do they let it drive them to despair or to dependence? Do they let it make them bitter or better? Do they let it become an excuse or an opportunity?

When you choose to let your weakness drive you to God instead of away from Him, you're making the most powerful choice you can make. When you decide to be honest about your struggles instead of hiding them, you're positioning yourself for a breakthrough. When you admit you need help instead of pretending you don't, you open the door for God's strength to show up in ways you never imagined.

Closing Reflection

Brother, if you're doing things you hate, you're not alone. If you're tired of falling, take heart, even Paul fell. But he didn't stay down. This fight you're in? It's proof you're alive. Proof you haven't given up.

The goal isn't to never struggle, the goal is to keep turning toward God, even in the middle of the struggle.

Your demons don't disqualify you. But you've got to love yourself, and those around you, more than your demons.

Your weakness isn't your downfall. It's your weapon. Use it. Let it drive you to God. Let it make you real. Let it become the very thing that transforms not just your life, but the lives of everyone you touch.

Stop running from your weakness. Start running with it, straight into the arms of the God who says,

"My grace is sufficient for you, for My strength is made perfect in weakness."

Prayer

Father, I confess that I've been trying to be strong in my own power.

I've been hiding my struggles, pretending I have it all together, and pushing away the very help I need.

Today I surrender my need to appear strong and embrace

Your strength that is made perfect in my weakness. Help me to see my struggles not as failures but as opportunities for

Your grace to show up. Give me the courage to be real, the wisdom to ask for help, and the faith to trust that Your grace is sufficient for every battle I face.

Use my weakness as a weapon for Your glory. In Jesus' name, Amen.

William "King" Hollis

Journaling Prompts

- What area of my life have I been trying to handle in my own strength?
- What would it look like to give that to God today?
- Where have I been hiding my struggles instead of bringing them to God?
- How has my fear of appearing weak actually made me weaker?
- What would change in my life if I truly believed that God's strength is made perfect in my weakness?

CHAPTER 3: Loving Through The Storm

"Above all, love each other deeply, because love covers over a multitude of sins."

– 1 Peter 4:8

Introduction: Loving When It's Not Easy

It's easy to love someone when the skies are clear and the sun is shining, when they agree with you, when they're emotionally stable, when they're giving back. In those moments, love flows effortlessly.

But the real test of love comes in the storm. When they're moody. When they shut down. When they hurt you. When they self-sabotage. When they push you away because they don't know how to receive real love.

That's when love stops being a feeling and becomes a decision.

Peter tells us, "Above all, love each other deeply." Not shallow love. Not convenient love. Not "as long as it benefits me" love. Deep love.

And why? Because it covers a multitude of sins. That doesn't mean it excuses or ignores wrongdoing, it means love holds on when everything else says to walk away.

This is one of the most soul-baring, transformative truths in Scripture:

The power of deep love to remain steady even when everything else is shaking.

It's about loving someone more than their demons, including the people in your life who are fighting battles you can't see, carrying burdens you don't understand, and wrestling with pain that causes them to act in ways that hurt both you and themselves.

What the Storm Reveals

Storms don't just shake relationships, they reveal them. A storm exposes what's real, what's fragile, and what still needs healing. Often, when someone is weathering a storm, their worst behaviors rise to the surface. They might lash out, withdraw, say things they don't mean, or do things they later regret. This is where most people walk away.

But a man rooted in love, God's love, doesn't flinch. He doesn't enable destructive behavior, but he also doesn't abandon the person. Instead, he becomes a shelter in the chaos.

Here's the truth: when people are in crisis, they rarely become better versions of themselves right away. More often, they become worse before they begin to heal. Pressure reveals the cracks. Pain exposes unhealed wounds. Fear activates the defense mechanisms they've built over years of trying to protect themselves from hurt.

And here's what most men don't understand: when someone you love is at their worst, that's often when they need your love the most, not your judgment, not your lectures, and not your attempts to fix them. What they need is your love, deep, consistent, unwavering love that says, "I'm not going anywhere, even when you're like this."

That doesn't mean becoming a doormat. It doesn't mean enabling destructive behavior. And it certainly doesn't mean sacrificing your own peace or well-being. But it does mean recognizing that their behavior is often a reflection of their pain, not their heart.

Think of it this way: when you're in physical pain, you don't act like your usual self. You might be irritable, impatient, even short with the people you care about. Pain alters the way you respond to the world. Emotional and spiritual pain do the same. When someone is deeply hurting, they often hurt others, not because they want to, but because hurt people hurt people.

Here's what love does: love sees past the behavior to the pain beneath it. Love understands that the lashing out comes from a wounded place. Love realizes that the pushing away is often a test, to see if you'll stay when things get hard.

What Does "Love Covers" Mean?

To cover means to protect, not to excuse. It says, "I see your worst, and I'm not running." It says, "I won't throw your sin in your face when you're already drowning." It says, "I'll hold the line for you while you find your way back."

That kind of love is rare, but it's also revolutionary. It doesn't mean accepting abuse or betraying your own peace. It means loving in a way that creates space for redemption, not just punishment. Because love that only shows up when someone's doing right isn't love at all.

When the Bible says love covers a multitude of sins, it's not about pretending sin doesn't exist or sweeping problems under the rug. It's about love that's strong enough to hold on when someone is at their worst. It's about love that refuses to give up on people, even when they've given up on themselves.

Most relationships operate on a performance basis: as long as you're meeting my needs, treating me well, and making me happy, I'll love you. But the moment you disappoint me, hurt me, or let me down, my love begins to withdraw. That's not biblical love, that's conditional acceptance.

God's love doesn't work that way. His love doesn't fluctuate based on our performance. It doesn't decrease when we mess up. It doesn't abandon us when we're at our worst. And He calls us to love others in the same way.

But here's what this kind of love requires: It requires being secure in your identity. It requires being rooted in God's love for you. It requires understanding that your worth doesn't come from how others treat you. Because if you're not secure in who you are, you'll seek validation through the behavior of others.

When you're grounded in God's love, you can love others from a place of overflow instead of need. You can give love without demanding it in return. You can offer grace without keeping score. You can extend mercy because you've received mercy.

Loving Through Their Demons

If you're reading this, chances are you've had to love someone battling their own demons, maybe addiction, depression, shame, pride, or fear. And maybe you've asked:

"How do I love someone who keeps hurting me? How do I love someone who doesn't even love themselves?"

Here's the truth:

- You love them by not becoming what hurt you.
- You love them by being an example, not a mirror.
- You love them by staying anchored in who you are, not who they are at their lowest.
- You don't let their storm pull you under, but you don't abandon ship either.
- You stay prayed up, full of wisdom, led by God, and rooted in truthful love.

See, when someone is battling demons, whether it's addiction, depression, trauma, or anything else, those demons don't just affect them. They affect everyone around them.

The addiction doesn't just wound the addict, it wounds the family.

The depression doesn't just weigh down the person, it weighs on their relationships.

The trauma doesn't just scar the victim, it reaches everyone who loves them.

And here's what happens:

Those demons will try to use the person you love to push you away.

They'll whisper lies that make them believe they're unworthy of love.

They'll stir up chaos to "prove" no one will stay.

They'll use shame to convince them they need to isolate to protect others from their mess.

But when you choose to love someone through their demons, you're not just loving the person, you're entering a spiritual battle with them.

You're refusing to let the enemy use their struggle to destroy your relationship.

You're standing in the gap when they can't stand on their own.

This is spiritual warfare at its most personal level. The enemy wants to use their demons to drive away everyone who cares, leaving them isolated and hopeless.

But when you choose to love them through the storm, you're partnering with God to break the cycle of destruction.

But let me be clear, this doesn't mean enabling destructive behavior.

It doesn't mean making excuses for choices that hurt you or others.

It doesn't mean sacrificing your well-being to hold onto someone who won't fight for their healing.

Loving someone through their demons means loving them enough not to participate in their destruction.

Loving them enough to set boundaries that protect you both. Loving them enough to speak truth, even when it hurts.

Loving them enough to keep praying, even when you can't be near them.

Why Love Is So Powerful

The world tells us that power is control. But God tells us the greatest power is love, because love heals what counseling can't touch. Love breaks chains that logic can't shatter. Love speaks life where words once destroyed. Love makes a man lay down his pride and pick up responsibility.

Love doesn't always "fix" people, but it gives them a reason to want to become better. That's what God's love did for us. He didn't wait for us to get it right, He loved us while we were still a mess. And when you love like that, through the storms, through the sin, through the silence, you're loving like Him.

Think about the most powerful transformations you've ever witnessed. Think about the people who've made the most dramatic, positive changes in their lives. Almost always, there was someone who loved them through their darkest moments, someone who saw their potential when they couldn't see it themselves. Someone who refused to give up on them, even when they had given up on themselves.

That's the power of love. It doesn't just accept people as they are, it calls them to become who they're meant to be. It doesn't just tolerate their present condition, it invites them into transformation. It doesn't just endure their weakness, it empowers them to find strength.

But this kind of love requires sacrifice. It requires you to die to your need to be right, to be appreciated, to be understood. It requires you to lay down your ego, your pride, your craving for immediate gratification. It asks you to invest in someone else's healing, even when it costs you something.

Most people aren't willing to love at this level because it's expensive. It costs time, energy, emotional labor, and sometimes even material resources. It demands patience when you crave quick results. It demands hope when the situation looks hopeless. It demands faith when there's no visible evidence of change.

But here's what you get in return: You get to participate in God's redemptive work in someone's life. You get to be a vessel through which His love flows. You get to witness the miraculous power of unconditional love to transform human hearts. You get to be part of someone's rescue story.

And often, in the process of loving someone else through their demons, you discover healing for your own. In extending grace, you receive grace. In choosing to forgive, you find freedom. And in deciding to love unconditionally, you experience the depth of God's love for you in ways you never understood before.

Boundaries and Grace

Let's be clear: loving someone deeply doesn't mean tolerating abuse, disrespect, or chaos. You can love someone with boundaries. In fact, genuine love requires them.

You can say:

"I love you, but I won't let you destroy me while you destroy yourself."

"I'm here for you, but I won't continue participating in the patterns that are killing you."

"I'm still praying for you, but I can't carry what only God can heal."

That's not giving up on them, that's entrusting them to God. This is where many people misunderstand biblical love. They believe loving someone means accepting whatever treatment they give. They assume grace means having no boundaries. They equate forgiveness with allowing continued harm.

But that's not love, that's enabling. That's not grace, that's foolishness. That's not forgiveness, that's self-destruction.

Real love sometimes says no. Real love sometimes walks away. Real love sometimes refuses to participate in someone else's self-destruction, not because you don't care, but because you care too much to watch them destroy themselves and everyone around them.

Boundaries aren't walls, they're gates. They don't shut people out; they create safe spaces for healthy relationships. They don't reject people; they protect both parties from harm. They don't end love; they define how love can be expressed in safe, constructive ways.

When you set boundaries with someone you love who's struggling, you're actually loving them on the deepest level. You're refusing to enable their destructive behavior. You're giving them the space to face the consequences of their choices. You're protecting the relationship from being consumed by their chaos.

But boundaries must come from a place of love, not anger. They must be established for protection, not punishment. They must be maintained with hope for restoration, not resignation to permanent separation.

And here's the crucial part: boundaries require follow-through. If you set a boundary but fail to uphold it, you're not protecting anyone, you're simply making empty threats. If you say you won't tolerate certain behavior but continue to accept it, you're teaching the other person that your words have no weight.

This is often the hardest part of loving someone through their demons. It requires the strength to enforce the boundaries you set, even when it breaks your heart. It demands that you love them enough to let them feel the pain of their choices, even when every part of you wants to shield them from the consequences.

Love Like Jesus, Not Like the World

The world says, "Cut them off." Jesus says, "Love them deeply." The world says, "Protect your pride." Jesus says, "Cover them in love."

Brother, if you want to be a man after God's own heart, then love can't be conditional. It must be rooted, resilient, and real. And when it's time to walk away, it should still be done in love, not bitterness. Because love never loses, even when it lets go.

The world has taught us a counterfeit version of love. It tells us love is primarily a feeling, that it should be easy, that it should always make us happy, and that we should abandon it when it gets hard. But that's not biblical love.

Biblical love is a choice, a commitment, a decision to seek someone's highest good, regardless of how they treat you. It's not dependent on feelings (though feelings may be involved). It's not always easy, but it's always worth it. It doesn't always make you happy, but it always makes you more like Christ.

Jesus loved His disciples even when they doubted Him. He loved Peter after Peter denied Him. He loved Judas, even though Judas betrayed Him. He loved the crowds even when they rejected Him. He loved His enemies, even as they crucified Him.

That's the standard of love we're called to. Not perfect love, none of us can love perfectly this side of heaven, but intentional love. Love that chooses to see people through God's eyes. Love that believes in people's potential, even when they can't see it themselves. Love that hopes for redemption, even in the darkest moments.

This doesn't mean you'll always feel loving toward those who hurt you. It doesn't mean you won't get angry, frustrated, or disappointed. And it doesn't mean you'll never need to take a step back from certain relationships to protect your emotional health.

But it does mean that underneath all the human emotions and natural reactions, there is a foundation of love that isn't shaken by circumstances. There's a commitment to seek their good, even when they aren't seeking yours. There's a hope for their healing, even when they're causing you pain.

When you love like Jesus, you become a safe place for broken people to find healing. You become a source of hope for those who've lost hope. You become a reflection of God's love for those who've forgotten that God loves them.

And often, the love you extend to others in their darkest moments becomes the very thing that draws them back to God. Your willingness to love them when they feel unlovable reminds them of God's unconditional love. Your refusal to give up on them reflects God's refusal to give up on them.

Closing Reflection

Brother, if someone in your life is going through a storm right now, they need your love more than your judgment. They need your prayers more than your lectures.

Love Them More Than Your Demons

They need your presence more than your advice. They need you to stay steady while everything else is shaking.

This doesn't mean you should become a doormat. It doesn't mean you should accept abuse. It doesn't mean you should enable destructive behavior. But it does mean you choose to love deeply, even when it's hard. It means you choose to cover them with love, even when they're at their worst. It means you choose to be an anchor in their storm, even when their waves threaten to pull you under.

Remember, you're not loving them with your own strength. You're loving them with God's love flowing through you. You're not covering their sins with your limited grace, you're extending God's unlimited grace through your life. You're not holding the line with your own power, you're partnering with the One who holds all things together.

And when it gets hard, and it will remember this: it's exactly how God loved you. When you were at your worst, He didn't abandon you. When you pushed Him away, He didn't give up. When you were battling your own demons, He covered you with His love.

Now He's asking you to do the same for others. Not because it's easy, but because it's powerful. Not because they deserve it, but because love isn't about what people deserve, it's about what God has freely given.

So love them through the storm. Cover them in the chaos. Hold the line when everything else is falling apart. Because love never fails, even when everything else does.

Prayer

God, help me love deeply, not just when it's easy, but when it's hard. Teach me how to cover, not control.

Help me to be a vessel of Your grace, even in the middle of their storm.

Give me wisdom to know when to hold on and when to let go, when to speak and when to be silent, when to stay close and when to love from a distance.

And when I get tired, remind me that Your love is what covered me first.

Help me love like You love unconditionally, sacrificially, and powerfully. In Jesus' name, amen.

William "King" Hollis

Journaling Prompts

- Who in your life is in a storm right now that needs your love more than your judgment?
- What does deep love look like in your current relationships?
- Are you loving people from a healed place or from fear of being left?
- How can you better balance boundaries and grace in your relationships?
- What would it look like to love someone the way God has loved you through your worst moments?

CHAPTER 4: Confronting The Inner Critic

"There is therefore now no condemnation to them which are in Christ Jesus."

– Romans 8:1

Introduction: You Ever Wondered If Grace Was Really For You?

Let's keep it real. Have you ever heard a scripture so good it almost feels like it couldn't apply to you? You read, "No condemnation..." and something deep inside says, "Yeah, but not for me. Not after what I've done."

Maybe you've let too many people down. Maybe you've been running from God for years. Maybe you've relapsed, lied, cheated, ghosted, or just flat-out given up on yourself.

But Romans 8:1 doesn't come with exceptions.

It doesn't say, "No condemnation for the perfect." It doesn't say, "No condemnation if you only mess up a little."

It doesn't say, "No condemnation unless you've already had too many chances."

It says:

NO CONDEMNATION for those who are in Christ Jesus. Period. That means you, not the future, polished version of you.

The present you: flawed, healing, still struggling. This is one of the most liberating verses in the Bible. But many men don't feel worthy of it, because they're still carrying shame from the past.

Here's what you need to understand:

This verse isn't about your worthiness. It's about God's grace.

It's not about what you've done, it's about what Jesus has done.

Most men live under a constant weight of condemnation. They wake up every day burdened by yesterday's failures. They go to bed each night replaying their regrets.

They live in a constant state of spiritual anxiety, wondering:

Have I pushed God too far? Have I crossed the line that can't be uncrossed?

But that's not how God sees you. That's not how this relationship works. That's not what Romans 8:1 is telling you.

How Do You Know This Scripture Is for You?

It's simple. Ask yourself this: Have you accepted Jesus? Are you leaning on Him, even in your mess? Are you still trying to grow, even when you fall? Then this is for you.

Romans 8:1 isn't about how good you are, it's about how good God is. The word condemnation refers to a final sentence, judgment with no hope of redemption. But when you're in Christ, your sentence isn't reduced; it's erased. You're no longer walking toward punishment, you're walking toward purpose.

Let me tell you why so many men struggle to receive this truth: We've been conditioned to believe that love and acceptance are earned. We've learned that approval always comes with conditions. We've been taught that when we mess up, we must earn our way back into good standing.

That might be how human relationships work, but that's not how your relationship with God works. God's love for you isn't based on performance. His acceptance isn't dependent on your behavior. His grace isn't limited by your failures.

When Romans 8:1 says no condemnation, it means exactly that. No condemnation for the man who keeps struggling with the same sin. No condemnation for the man who feels like he's taking two steps forward and three steps back. No condemnation for the man who's tired of letting people down. No condemnation for the man who feels like he'll never get it right.

You are in Christ Jesus. That's your identity. That's your position. That's your reality. And nothing you do, or fail to do can change that truth.

Condemnation vs. Conviction: Knowing the Difference

This is where most men get stuck. You make a mistake, and immediately that all-too-familiar voice creeps in:

"You'll never change." "You're a disappointment." "You're too far gone." "God's tired of you."

That's not conviction, that's shame. And shame is the enemy's native language. Let's break it down:

Condemnation (from the Enemy):

You're a failure, Hide. Don't talk about it, you'll never be free, God's done with you, Guilt with no end

Conviction (from God):

You made a mistake, but you're still my son, Bring it into the light. Let Me heal it, I died to set you free, keep walking, I'm still here. Let's start again, Correction with love.

God corrects sons, not strangers. Hebrews 12:6 says, "The Lord disciplines those He loves..." Conviction is God saying, "You're better than this, and I'm not giving up on you."

When you feel convicted, don't run lean in. It's proof you haven't been abandoned. God is still shaping you. That tension in your spirit isn't rejection it's refinement.

Conviction only exists within a relationship. And Romans 8:1 reminds us that the relationship isn't over just because you fell short.

The enemy wants you to confuse conviction with condemnation, because he knows that if you can't tell the difference, you'll run from God when you should be running to Him. He wants you to believe that every time you feel bad about your sin, it's God rejecting you. But that's backwards.

The fact that you feel grief over your sin is actually evidence that God's Spirit is still working in you. Dead people don't feel guilt. Hardened hearts don't experience conviction. The very fact that your failures bother you means you are still alive spiritually, still connected to God, and still being shaped by His love.

Why Shame Is So Dangerous

Shame doesn't just make you feel bad, it keeps you stuck. It whispers, "You might as well give up." "God's grace doesn't work for you." "You're too dirty to be used."

But shame is a liar.

God never asked you to be flawless, He asked you to be faithful. That means showing up even when you're broken. It means returning to Him even when you feel unworthy. Because if the enemy can keep you buried in shame, he can keep you from your assignment.

Shame is one of the enemy's most effective weapons because it doesn't just attack what you've done, it attacks who you are.

Sin says, "I did something bad."

Shame says, "I am something bad."

Sin can be forgiven and cleansed. But shame tries to convince you that you are the problem, that you're irredeemably broken, beyond hope.

But here's what shame doesn't want you to know: it has no power over someone who understands Romans 8:1. Shame can only control you if you believe its lies about your identity. But when you know that there is no condemnation for those who are in Christ Jesus, shame loses its grip.

The enemy uses shame to keep you isolated. He knows that if you're carrying shame, you'll avoid the very things that bring healing.

You won't want to be around other believers. You won't want to go to church. You won't want to pray. You won't want to read your Bible.

Why? Because shame tells you that you don't deserve them. But Romans 8:1 crushes that lie.

It reminds you that your access to God isn't based on performance, it's based on your position in Christ. Your worth isn't determined by your behavior, it's defined by Jesus' sacrifice. Your acceptance isn't conditional on your goodness, it's secured by His grace.

The Truth About Grace

Grace doesn't mean sin doesn't matter, it means you don't have to be defined by it. Grace isn't permission to live messy; it's power to live free.

So when you mess up and you will, don't sink into silence. Don't ghost God. Don't cancel yourself. Remember: "There is therefore now no condemnation..." Not "someday." Not after a 30-day perfect record. Now.

Grace is perhaps the most misunderstood concept in Christianity, especially among men. Some believe grace means God doesn't care about sin. Others see it as a get-out-of-jail-free card that lets you live however you want. But that's not biblical grace.

Biblical grace is unmerited favor, but it's also God's empowering presence. Grace doesn't just forgive your past;

it transforms your future. It doesn't just cover your sin; it gives you power over sin. It doesn't just save you from hell; it rescues you from hopelessness.

When you truly understand grace, it doesn't make you want to sin more, it makes you want to sin less. Not because you're afraid of punishment, but because you're grateful for the gift. Not because you need to earn God's love, but because you've already received it.

Grace teaches you that your failures don't define you, but they don't have to defeat you either. It reminds you that while you're not perfect, you are loved. While you're not finished, you are forgiven. And while you're not where you want to be, you're not where you used to be.

And here's what grace does for a man: It gives him permission to be honest about his struggles without fear of rejection. It gives him hope that change is possible, even when it feels impossible. It gives him strength to keep fighting, even when he feels like giving up.

A Word to the Man Who Feels Like He Blew It

If you feel like this scripture couldn't possibly apply to you, let me tell you this:

If you've lied, it still applies to you. If you've fallen back into sin, it still applies to you.

If you're struggling to believe you'll ever change, this scripture is your anchor.

God knew every mistake you would ever make, and He still sent Jesus to clear your record.

So walk like a man who's been pardoned, not like a man still waiting on a verdict.

Maybe you're reading this and thinking, "You don't understand what I've done. You don't know how far I've fallen. You don't know how many times I've failed."

But here's what I want you to know: God does understand.

He knows every failure, every mistake, every moment of weakness.

And He still says, "No condemnation."

- Do you think your sin surprised God?
- Do you think your failure caught Him off guard?

- Do you believe your struggle is greater than His grace?

The God who created the universe, who knows the end from the beginning, who sees all things, He knew exactly who He was choosing when He chose you.

And He chose you anyway. The cross wasn't Plan B.

Grace wasn't God's backup plan when He saw how broken humanity would be.

From the foundation of the world, God knew we would fall, and from the foundation of the world, He had already planned to redeem us.

Your sin didn't force God to come up with a new strategy.

Your failure didn't make Him adjust His plan.

God's love for you isn't based on your potential, it's rooted in His character.

His grace toward you isn't dependent on your performance, it's anchored in His nature.

His acceptance of you isn't conditional on your improvement, it's secured by Jesus' sacrifice.

So stop carrying guilt that Jesus already carried. Stop punishing yourself for sins God has already forgiven.

Stop living under condemnation that Christ has already removed.

Walking in Freedom

When you truly believe Romans 8:1, it changes everything. It changes how you approach God when you've messed up. Instead of hiding in shame, you come to Him honestly. Instead of carrying guilt, you receive grace. Instead of living in fear of rejection, you rest in His acceptance.

It transforms how you see yourself. You stop identifying as a failure and start seeing yourself as a son. You stop seeing yourself as condemned and start recognizing that you are chosen. You stop believing lies about your worth and begin believing the truth about your identity.

It reshapes how you pursue spiritual growth. You stop trying to earn God's love and start responding to it. You stop striving for acceptance and begin living from a place of acceptance. You stop working to become worthy and start working because you already are loved.

And it changes how you relate to others. When you're secure in God's acceptance, you can extend grace to others. When you know you're loved unconditionally, you can love without conditions. When you realize you've been forgiven much, you can forgive much.

But walking in this freedom requires daily choices. Every day, you must choose to believe Romans 8:1 over the voice of shame. Every day, you must choose grace over guilt. Every day, you must choose to walk as a son, not a slave.

The enemy will keep trying to convince you that you're condemned. Your past will try to define your future. Your failures will try to disqualify you from God's love. But you have a powerful weapon against all of these lies: the truth of Romans 8:1.

Closing Declaration

Brother, I want you to say this out loud:

"I am no longer under condemnation. I walk in conviction, not shame. I'm not perfect, but I'm covered. I will not let the enemy convince me to carry guilt I am forgiven. I am free. I am His."

This scripture is for you, not because you're perfect, but because you're in Christ.

Not because you deserve it, but because grace isn't about what you deserve.

Not because you'll never fail again, but because failure doesn't have the final word.

You are not condemned. You are not rejected. You are not disqualified. You are loved, chosen, and secure in Christ Jesus.

This isn't based on your performance, it's grounded in God's promise. And His promises don't change with your circumstances.

So when the enemy whispers condemnation, you declare Romans 8:1.

When shame tries to silence you, you proclaim your freedom.

When guilt tries to drag you down, you stand firm in who you are in Christ.

This is for you, all of it. Every word, every promise, every assurance.

You don't have to earn it, and you can't lose it. You simply have to receive it.

Prayer

Father, thank You that there is no condemnation for those who are in Christ Jesus.

Help me to truly believe this truth, not just in my head but in my heart.

When shame tries to convince me that I'm disqualified, remind me of my identity in You.

When guilt tries to separate me from Your love, help me remember that nothing can separate me from Your love.

Each me the difference between conviction and condemnation, and help me to run to You when I fail instead of running away.

Thank You for Your grace that covers all my failures and Your love that never gives up on me. In Jesus' name,

Amen.

William "King" Hollis

Journaling Prompts

- Am I carrying condemnation that God already forgave me for?
- Do I recognize the difference between God correcting me and the enemy shaming me?
- What does living "in Christ Jesus" look like in my day-to-day life? How would my life change if I truly believed that there is no condemnation for me?
- What lies about my identity do I need to replace with the truth of God's Word?

CHAPTER 5: Healing the Father Wound

"A father to the fatherless, a defender of widows, is God in his holy dwelling."

– Psalm 68:5

Introduction: Who Fills the Gap When a Father Isn't There?

Too many men grew up in homes where the father was either absent, abusive, or emotionally unavailable. Some never heard the words, "I'm proud of you." Some were never taught how to love a woman, how to fight for a family, or how to stand tall as men of integrity. Some watched their mothers carry burdens they were never meant to bear alone.

And deep down, many men still carry that silent pain, wondering: "If my own father didn't choose me… does that mean I'm unworthy?"

That's why Psalm 68:5 is so powerful. It reminds us: Even if your earthly father failed you, God did not. Even if no man ever showed up for you, God still does. Even if you grew up fatherless, you are not orphaned.

Because in His holy dwelling, God declares: "I will personally be a Father to the fatherless."

This verse is more than just a comforting phrase, it's a declaration of identity for the broken, a promise of protection for the abandoned, and a call to healing for every man who never had a father to model manhood. It hits deep, especially for men battling silent wounds that trace back to childhood.

The father wound is one of the deepest a man can carry. It affects how you see yourself, how you relate to authority, how you approach relationships, and how you understand your own worth. When a father fails to show up, physically, emotionally, or spiritually, it leaves a void many men spend their whole lives trying to fill.

Some try to fill it with work, chasing success to prove their value. Others pursue relationships, searching for the validation their fathers never gave. Some turn to anger, using rage to mask the pain of feeling unwanted. Others choose numbness, shutting down emotionally just to escape the ache of abandonment.

But none of these things can heal the father wound. Only knowing your true Father can.

Why This Scripture Is Critical for Healing

You can't become the man you were born to be until you heal the boy you used to be. If that boy inside you still feels abandoned, rejected, or forgotten, you'll keep bleeding on people who never cut you.

Psalm 68:5 offers men a new foundation. It says: "You didn't miss out on love, it was waiting for you in the Father." "You're not cursed, you're covered." "You don't have to repeat what you saw, you can walk in who you are."

The father wound doesn't just affect your relationship with men, it affects your relationship with God. Many men struggle to see God as a loving Father because their only reference point for fatherhood is broken. They project their earthly father's failures onto their heavenly Father, assuming God will disappoint them the same way their dad did.

But here's what you need to understand: God is not your earthly father. He doesn't carry your dad's limitations, your dad's wounds, or his inability to love consistently. God is the perfect Father every man longs for but few experience in earthly relationships.

When your earthly father failed you, it wasn't because you weren't worth loving, it was because he was broken too. Hurt people hurt people. Absent people abandon people. Your father's inability to show up for you says nothing about your worth, and everything about his wounds.

But God's fatherhood is different. His love isn't conditional on your performance. His presence doesn't depend on His mood. His commitment to you isn't shaped by unresolved issues. He is the Father who never leaves, never disappoints, never gives up, and never stops believing in who you can become.

What It Means to Call God "Father"

Most men don't know how to relate to God as a Father, because "father" is a wounded word. If your earthly father was violent, distant, or absent, then "Father" might feel more like punishment than protection.

But here's the truth: God doesn't walk away, He stays. God doesn't punish you for crying, He holds you while you cry. God doesn't make you earn love, He gives it freely.

Calling God your Father doesn't mean pretending your earthly father didn't fail you. It means healing that wound by turning to the true source of strength.

When you begin to understand God as your true Father, everything changes. You stop looking for validation from people who can't give it. You stop trying to earn love from a source that has already offered it without condition. You stop living from a place of abandonment and begin living from a place of acceptance.

But this transformation isn't easy, especially if you've been hurt deeply by the man who was meant to protect and provide for you. It requires risking the belief that fatherhood can be different from what you experienced. It asks you to open your heart to a love that feels too good to be true, especially when your only reference was love that was conditional, inconsistent, or entirely absent.

The enemy wants to use your father wound to keep you from experiencing God's fatherhood. He wants you to believe that all fathers are unreliable, that all love comes with strings attached, that all relationships end in disappointment. He wants your earthly father's failures to become a barrier between you and your heavenly Father's love.

But God's fatherhood isn't like human fatherhood. Human fathers are limited, by their own wounds, their capacity, their understanding. But God's fatherhood is limitless, unconditional, and perfect. He never has a bad day that affects how He treats you. He never becomes overwhelmed by His problems and forgets about yours. He never withdraws His love because He's dealing with His own pain.

The Father You Never Had

Let me paint a picture of the Father you have in God, the Father you may have never encountered in human form:

This Father celebrates your victories without claiming the credit.

This Father comforts you in failure without condemning you for it.

This Father believes in your potential, even when you can't see it yourself.

This Father protects you, even when you don't realize you need protection.

This Father provides for you, often before you even think to ask.

This Father doesn't compare you to anyone else, He delights in who you are uniquely.

This Father doesn't withhold affection to teach lessons, He lavishes love to anchor your identity.

This Father doesn't abandon you when you fall short, He draws closer to walk you through the struggle.

This Father knows your name, your dreams, your fears, and your future.

This Father sees not just who you are, but who you're becoming.

This Father doesn't merely tolerate you, He delights in you.

This Father doesn't just meet your needs, He finds joy in blessing you.

This is the Father Psalm 68:5 speaks of.

This is the Father who stepped in when your earthly father stepped out.

This is the Father who's been waiting for you to realize, you're not fatherless.

You're just now learning who your real Father is.

How to Apply This Scripture in Real Life

Here's how men can begin to live this verse, even if they never had a father to teach them:

Talk to God Like a Father, Not Just a Distant King
Start your prayers with "Father, I need You..."

Not because it sounds religious, but because it builds a real, personal connection. You don't have to come perfect, you just have to come real. Ask Him the questions you never had the chance to ask your dad. Ask Him how to be a man, how to lead, how to let go.

Too often, men pray to God as if He's a distant authority figure who might help if they ask politely enough. But that's not how sons relate to fathers. Sons bring their real needs, their honest questions, their deepest fears. They don't perform for their fathers, they trust them.

Talk to God the way you always wished you could have talked to your earthly father. Tell Him about your day. Ask for advice. Share your struggles without trying to clean them up first. Thank Him for the ways He's already shown up in your life. Complain when life feels unfair.

This is how sons relate to fathers, with honesty, trust, and intimacy.

Release the Image of the Man Who Hurt You

You can't embrace God as Father while still worshipping, or resenting, a broken version of one.

Forgiveness doesn't excuse what your dad did; it frees you from carrying it. Let the pain go, so you can finally grow.

This is often the hardest part of healing the father wound. You have to release your earthly father from the debt he owes you. Stop waiting for him to become the man he should have been. Forgive him for what he didn't give you, so you can receive what God wants to.

Forgiveness doesn't mean pretending the hurt didn't happen. It doesn't mean minimizing the impact of his failures. It doesn't mean putting yourself back in a place where you can be hurt again.

It means no longer letting his shortcomings define your future.

Forgiveness isn't about your father, it's about your freedom. As long as you're holding on to bitterness, resentment, or the hope that he'll change and become the father you needed, you're not free to receive the fatherhood God longs to give you.

Step Into Sonship

Being a son of God isn't a sign of weakness, it's the most powerful identity you can walk in. It means you're covered, even when you stumble. You're corrected with love, not rejection. You have access to divine wisdom, strength, and direction. You're no longer winging manhood, you have a Father guiding your every step.

Sonship is more than just being forgiven, it's about being welcomed into God's family. It means having access to everything that belongs to your Father. It's about being loved, not just despite your flaws, but because of your identity as His child.

When you truly understand sonship, you stop trying to earn God's love and start enjoying it. You stop striving for acceptance and begin living from a place of it. You stop trying to prove your worth and start living from the worth He's already given you.

But sonship also comes with responsibility. Sons represent their fathers. Sons carry on their fathers' legacy. Sons learn their fathers' ways and follow their example. When you embrace sonship with God, you're not just receiving His love, you're committing to live in a way that honors His name.

Become What You Didn't Have

If you grew up without a father, then be the man your younger self needed. Be the father your children, mentees, or community can count on. You are not defined by what you lacked, you are defined by what you choose to give. God fills you so that you can pour into others.

One of the most powerful ways to heal from a father wound is to become the father you wish you had, not just to your biological children, but also to the next generation of men searching for someone to show them what godly manhood looks like.

This doesn't mean you have to be perfect. It doesn't mean you need to have everything figured out. But it does mean you can break the cycle. You can be the man who shows up. The man who affirms and encourages. The man who teaches by example what it looks like to love God, love your family, and live with integrity.

When you become what you didn't have, you're not just healing your own wound, you're helping prevent that wound in someone else. You're breaking the generational pattern of absent, abusive, or emotionally unavailable fathers. You're becoming part of the solution instead of continuing the problem.

Why This Matters Now

So many men are hurting silently because they've never seen God as a Father who stays, a protector who defends, or a healer who holds. But this Scripture reminds us that God is not intimidated by your pain, He steps into it. He sits with you in it. And He speaks truth to the parts of you that feel abandoned.

Psalm 68:5 isn't just comfort, it's identity. You are not fatherless. You are not forgotten. You are not finished.

The father wound touches every part of a man's life. It shapes how he sees himself, how he relates to authority, how he approaches relationships, how he fathers his own children, and how he understands his purpose and calling. But when a man discovers that he has a Father in heaven who loves him unconditionally, everything changes.

He stops seeking validation from those who can't give it. He stops trying to prove his worth through performance. He stops carrying the shame of feeling unwanted or unworthy. Instead, he begins to live from a place of security instead of insecurity, acceptance instead of rejection, and love instead of fear.

This transformation doesn't happen overnight. The father wound runs deep, and healing takes time. But it begins with believing the truth of Psalm 68:5, that God is a Father to the fatherless, and that includes you.

Living as a Son

When you truly embrace your identity as God's son, it transforms how you approach every part of life. You pray with confidence, knowing your Father hears you. You face challenges with courage, knowing your Father is fighting for you. You love others freely because you're secure in your Father's love.

You stop trying to earn acceptance and begin living from a place of acceptance. You stop striving for love and start acting out of love. You stop fighting for your worth and begin fighting from your worth.

But living as a son also means being open to correction. Good fathers discipline their children, not to punish them, but to protect and guide them toward their best life. When God corrects you, it's not out of anger; it's out of love. He loves you too much to let you remain stuck in patterns that could harm you.

Sons trust their fathers even when they don't fully understand their decisions. Sons believe their fathers have their best interests at heart, even when the road is hard. Sons know their fathers' love isn't dependent on circumstances..

Breaking the Cycle

One of the most powerful truths about understanding God as your Father is that it gives you the strength to break generational cycles. Maybe your father was absent because his father was absent. Maybe he was abusive because his father was abusive. Maybe he was emotionally unavailable because that's all he ever knew.

But when you come to know your true Father in God, you gain the power to choose a different path. You have the strength to become the father your children need. You have the wisdom to be the mentor other men are searching for. You have the courage to model healthy masculinity for the next generation.

This is how generational healing begins, one man at a time deciding to be more than what he experienced. One man at a time choosing to break the cycle instead of repeating it. One man at a time discovering that he has a Father in heaven who can teach him what his earthly father could not.

Closing Reflection

Brother, if you grew up without a father, or if your father failed to be the man you needed him to be, I want you to know this: you are not doomed to repeat his mistakes. You're not destined to carry the same wounds forever. You are not cursed because of what you didn't receive.

You have a Father in heaven who sees you, knows you, loves you, and is proud of you. He's been waiting for you to realize that you're not an orphan, you're a son. He's been longing for you to understand that you're not fatherless, you just hadn't met your true Father yet.

This Father will never leave you. This Father will never disappoint you. This Father will never stop believing in who you can become.

He will teach you everything you need to know about being a man, about loving others, and about living with purpose and integrity.

You are not fatherless. You are not forgotten. You are not finished.

You are a son of the Most High God, and that changes everything.

Prayer

Father, thank You for stepping in where others stepped out.

Thank You for defending me, loving me, and never giving up on me.

Heal every broken piece in me that still feels fatherless. Help me to see You not through the lens of my earthly father's failures, but through the truth of Your perfect love.

Raise up the man You created me to be one who loves, leads, and lifts others with the same grace You've given me.

Teach me how to be a son, and help me to become the father that others need.

I am Yours. I am a son.

I am not alone.

Amen.

William "King" Hollis

Journaling Prompts

- Have I ever truly seen God as a Father or just as a figure of fear and judgment?
- What parts of me still hurt from not having an earthly father show up?
- How would my life change if I believed God was always present, proud, and protective?
- What would it look like for me to step fully into my identity as God's son?
- How can I become the father figure for others that I needed when I was younger?

CHAPTER 6:
Forgiveness as a Weapon

"Be kind and compassionate to one another, forgiving each other, just as in Christ God forgave you."

– Ephesians 4:32

Introduction: Reading Heals the Mind Applying Heals the Heart

Brother, you didn't pick up this book just to get inspired,, you picked it up to get free. There's a difference between knowing the Word and living the Word. Between reading about forgiveness and actually forgiving those who hurt you. Between understanding compassion and showing it when your pride is screaming for revenge.

Ephesians 4:32 doesn't say, "Be kind if they deserve it." It doesn't say, "Forgive when you feel like it." It doesn't say, "Show compassion only to those who treat you right."

It says: Be kind. Be compassionate. Forgive, just as Christ forgave you. Not because it's easy. Not because they earned it. But because your peace depends on it.

This verse isn't just a suggestion, it's a strategy for healing. Forgiveness and compassion are keys to freedom, not just for the person you're forgiving, but for you. This chapter will show you why it's essential not just to read this book, but to live it, especially when it comes to letting go of past pain.

Up until now, we've been breaking down the problems, identifying the struggles, and understanding the battles. But now, it's time to get practical. It's time to do the work. Because knowledge without application is just spiritual entertainment. And understanding without action? That's just religious therapy. You can know every verse in the Bible about healing and still be the most wounded person in the room, if you never apply what you know.

Why This Verse Is a Call to Action

Every chapter in this book is meant to lead you toward healing. But this verse? It makes it clear that healing isn't passive, it's intentional. And it costs you something: ego, anger, pride, and sometimes the need to be right.

Forgiveness and compassion aren't weaknesses, they're weapons. Every time you forgive, you break a chain from your past. Every time you show compassion, you rebuild a bridge the enemy tried to burn. Ephesians 4:32 is your instruction manual for becoming a healed man, not just a hurting one with wisdom.

See, most men approach healing as if it's something that simply happens to them, rather than something they actively engage in. They read books about forgiveness and wait to feel forgiving. They learn about compassion and wait for it to naturally arise. They understand grace and expect it to flow through them automatically.

But that's not how spiritual growth works. That's not how healing happens. That's not how transformation occurs. Healing demands your participation. It calls for choices that feel unnatural, decisions that challenge your flesh, and actions that contradict your emotions.

The enemy wants you to believe that if forgiveness were real, it would feel easy. He wants you to think that if compassion were genuine, it would come naturally. He wants you to assume that if healing were God's will, it would happen automatically. But that's not biblical thinking, that's passive thinking.

Biblical healing is active. It calls you to choose forgiveness when you feel angry. It asks you to show compassion when you want revenge. It requires you to be kind when everything in you wants to turn cold. It pushes you to do the right thing, even when you don't feel like doing the right thing.

Why It's Not Optional

You may be thinking: "Why should I forgive someone who isn't sorry? Why should I be kind to the person who used me? Why should I care about their feelings when they ignored mine?"

Here's why: Because Jesus did it for you. He forgave you before you ever changed. He loved you while you were still sinning. He showed you kindness even as you were rejecting Him. And if you're in Christ, you're called to reflect that same mercy.

This isn't just about being nice. It's not just about keeping the peace. It's not even about being the bigger person. It's about walking in the same spirit that saved you. It's about extending the same grace that rescued you. It's about offering others what you once received when you didn't deserve it.

But here's what most men miss: forgiveness isn't primarily about the other person, it's about you. Compassion isn't mainly for their benefit, it's for your freedom. Kindness isn't just about making them feel better, it's about keeping your heart soft.

When you refuse to forgive, you're not punishing them, you're imprisoning yourself. When you withhold compassion, you're not protecting yourself, you're hardening your heart. When you choose bitterness over kindness, you're not staying strong, you're becoming what hurt you.

The people who hurt you have likely moved on. They're probably not thinking about what they did to you. They're not losing sleep over your pain. But if you're holding on to unforgiveness, you are the one still suffering. You are the one still carrying the weight. You are the one still paying the price for their choices.

What Happens When You Don't Forgive

Let's be real: unforgiveness poisons your peace, hardens your heart, clouds your thinking, and pushes away the very people God sent to bless you. Holding onto bitterness doesn't hurt them, it hurts you. You become guarded. Suspicious. Cold. Isolated. You begin to see the world through your pain instead of your purpose.

But when you forgive, when you choose kindness and compassion, you begin to heal. You free yourself from becoming the very thing that broke you.

Unforgiveness is like drinking poison and expecting the other person to die. It's like gripping a burning coal with the intent to throw it at someone else, yet you're the one getting burned. It's like staying in a prison when the door is wide open, waiting for your offender to come unlock it.

When you hold onto unforgiveness, you hand over power, power over your present and your future. You let their past actions control your current emotions. You allow their choices to dictate your peace. You permit their failures to define your freedom.

Worse still, unforgiveness reshapes who you are. It makes you suspicious of people who genuinely care. It turns you cold toward those who want to love you. It makes you defensive with those trying to help. It hardens you when God is trying to keep your heart tender.

Unforgiveness doesn't just affect your relationship with the one who hurt you, it affects every relationship you have. It builds walls where God wants to build bridges. It creates distance where God wants to create intimacy. It breeds cynicism where God wants to grow hope.

Here's the tragic part: most of the time, the people you refuse to forgive don't even realize you're still angry. They've moved on. They've forgotten. They're living their lives while you're stuck reliving the pain they caused. You're giving them free rent in your mind while they don't even remember your address.

Compassion Isn't Coddling, It's Courage

To be kind in a cold world takes guts. To show compassion when everyone else is angry takes strength. To forgive someone who wounded you deeply takes God, and that's the point.

You can't do this on your own. But with Christ in you, you're empowered to walk in the same mercy He walked in. You become dangerous to the enemy because you're no longer controlled by offense.

Compassion doesn't mean you're weak, it means you're strong enough to be gentle.

Kindness doesn't mean you're a pushover, it means you're secure enough to remain soft.

Forgiveness doesn't mean you're naive, it means you're wise enough to let go.

The world will tell you that compassion is weakness, that kindness is foolishness, that forgiveness means being taken advantage of. But the world is wrong. It operates from fear, scarcity, and self-protection.

But you don't have to live by the world's values, you can live by God's.

God's values say that showing mercy is strength. God's values say that choosing love over hate is power. God's values say that being compassionate when you have every right to be angry is the highest form of spiritual maturity.

But here's what compassion doesn't mean:

It doesn't mean enabling destructive behavior. It doesn't mean putting yourself back in a position to be hurt. It doesn't mean pretending the offense never happened.

It doesn't mean trusting someone who hasn't proven trustworthy.

You can forgive and still set boundaries. You can show compassion and still protect your peace. You can be kind and still say no. You can extend grace and still require accountability.

Forgiveness doesn't erase consequences, it removes your need for revenge.

Compassion doesn't ignore justice, it trusts God with justice. Kindness doesn't accept abuse, it chooses love over hate, even while setting firm boundaries.

The Cost of Doing the Work

Let's be honest about what this work requires.

- Choosing forgiveness over bitterness will cost you the right to hold grudges.
- Choosing compassion over anger will cost you the energy you gain from rage.
- Choosing kindness over coldness will cost you the sense of protection that emotional walls provide.

This work will ask you to feel the pain you've been avoiding. It will ask you to acknowledge the hurt you've been denying. It will ask you to face emotions you've been numbing.

It will ask you to be vulnerable when you'd rather stay guarded.

This work will require you to release your victim story, not because your pain isn't real, but because your healing matters more than your hurt.

Not because what happened to you doesn't matter, but because what happens through you matters even more.

This work will call you to take responsibility for your healing, even when you weren't responsible for the wounding.

You didn't choose the pain, but you can choose to heal. You didn't ask to be hurt, but you can decide how to respond to the hurt.

This work will require you to love people who haven't earned it, to forgive people who don't deserve it, and to show compassion to people who might never appreciate it.

And you'll do it, not because they deserve it, but because you deserve to be free.

But here's what this work gives you in return:

It gives you your life back. It gives you your peace back. It gives you your joy back.

It restores your ability to trust again, to love again, to hope again.

When you do the work of forgiveness, you're not just setting others free, you're setting yourself free.

When you choose compassion over bitterness, you're not just blessing others, you're blessing yourself.

When you extend kindness instead of coldness, you're not just changing them, you're changing you.

Living This Chapter, Not Just Reading It

Here's the truth: None of the wisdom in this book will matter if you don't apply it. If you don't take time to reflect, you'll just be inspired but unchanged. If you don't do the hard inner work, forgive, heal, show compassion, the cycle will repeat. If you only read about healing, you'll never live in healing.

That's why every chapter ends with reflection. Because change doesn't happen when you turn the page, it happens when you turn inward.

Reading this book can inform your mind, but only applying this book can transform your life. You can have all the knowledge in the world about forgiveness, but if you never forgive, you'll still be bound. You can understand every principle about compassion, but if you never show compassion, you'll still be hard. You can know every truth about healing, but if you never do the work of healing, you'll still be wounded.

The enemy doesn't care if you read about transformation, he only cares if you actually transform. He's not threatened by your knowledge, he's threatened by your application. He's not worried about your understanding, he's worried about your obedience.

So the question isn't whether you understand what this chapter is saying. The question is whether you're willing to do what this chapter is asking. Are you willing to forgive the people who hurt you? Are you willing to show compassion to people who showed you none? Are you willing to be kind even when you don't feel like it? Here's the truth: none of the wisdom in this book will matter if you don't apply it. If you don't take time to reflect, you may feel inspired, but you'll remain unchanged. If you avoid the hard inner work, like forgiving, healing, and showing compassion, the cycle will repeat. If you only read about healing, you'll never experience healing.

That's why every chapter ends with reflection. Because change doesn't happen when you turn the page, it happens when you turn inward.

Reading this book can inform your mind, but only applying it can transform your life. You can have all the knowledge in the world about forgiveness, but if you never forgive, you'll remain bound. You can understand every principle about compassion, but if you never show it, your heart will stay hard. You can know every truth about healing, but if you never engage in the work of healing, you'll remain wounded.

The enemy doesn't care if you read about transformation, he cares if you actually transform. He's not threatened by your knowledge, he's threatened by your obedience. He's not worried about what you understand, he's worried about what you live.

So the question isn't whether you understand what this chapter is saying. The question is whether you're willing to do what this chapter is asking. Are you willing to forgive those who hurt you? Are you willing to show compassion to those who showed you none? Are you willing to be kind, even when you don't feel like it?

The Process of Forgiveness

Let me give you a practical framework for doing this work:

First, acknowledge the hurt. Don't minimize it. Don't spiritualize it. Don't rationalize it away. What they did was wrong. How they treated you was unacceptable. The pain you feel is real, and valid.

Second, feel the emotions. Don't rush past the anger, the sadness, the disappointment. Let yourself feel it fully so you can heal it completely. Emotions that aren't felt don't disappear, they go underground and influence your behavior in ways you might not even realize.

Third, choose to forgive. Forgiveness is a decision, not a feeling. You choose to release them from the debt they owe you. You choose to give up your right to revenge. You choose to let God handle the justice while you handle the forgiveness.

Fourth, speak the forgiveness. Say it out loud, either to them directly or to God in prayer: "I forgive [name] for [specific offense]. I release them from the debt they owe me. I choose to let go of my right to revenge."

Fifth, live the forgiveness. This means you stop rehearsing the offense. You stop retelling the story to gain sympathy. You stop using their failure as a justification for your dysfunction. You treat them as forgiven, even if they don't know they are.

This isn't a one-time event, it's a process. You may have to choose forgiveness more than once for the same offense. You may need to speak it repeatedly until your heart catches up with your words. You may have to live it daily until it becomes second nature.

The Power of Applied Scripture

When you live out Ephesians 4:32, you don't just read about God's poweryou demonstrate it.

When you forgive as Christ forgave you, you don't just speak about grace, you embody it.

When you show compassion to those who have hurt you, you don't just grasp the concept of mercy, you model it.

This is how Scripture becomes more than words on a page, it becomes a source of transformation.

This is how the Bible becomes more than a book you read, it becomes a life you live.

This is how faith becomes more than something you believe, it becomes something you practice.

And when you live this way, you become a walking testimony of God's power.

People witness your forgiveness and wonder how you're able to forgive like that.

They observe your compassion and are drawn to the source of that compassion.

They notice your kindness and want to understand what makes you different.

You become a living example of what it means to be healed, to be free, to be transformed by the love of God.

You become living proof that change is possible, that healing is real, and that God's grace is sufficient for every wound.

Closing Reflection

Don't just highlight this verse, live it. Don't just post about healing, pursue it. Don't just quote forgiveness, walk in it.

You were never meant to carry all that pain for a lifetime. Let it go, and watch what God can do through a healed man with a soft heart and a fearless spirit.

The work is hard, but the freedom is worth it. The process is painful, but the peace is real. The choice is difficult, but the change is lasting.

You have everything you need to do this work:

God's Spirit to guide you, His Word to direct you, and His grace to sustain you.

You have examples, others who have walked this path before you.

You have the promise that He who began a good work in you will complete it.

The only question left is: Will you do the work?

Declaration

"I am no longer a prisoner to pain.

I choose compassion over control, forgiveness over bitterness, and peace over pride.

I will walk in the freedom Christ died to give me I will love others like He first loved me."

Prayer

Father, give me the strength to do the work that needs to be done.

Help me to forgive like You forgave me completely, freely, without condition.

Help me to show compassion like You showed me compassion, abundantly, graciously, without reservation.

Help me to be kind like You were kind to me, patiently, consistently, without limit.

I choose to release those who have hurt me, not because they deserve it, but because I deserve to be free.

Transform my heart, heal my wounds, and use my story to help others find the same freedom

I'm walking in. In Jesus' name,

Amen

William "King" Hollis

Reflection Questions

Take a quiet moment with no distractions, no ego, just truth:

- Who do I still need to forgive, not for their sake, but for mine?
- What moment in my life hardened my heart and made kindness feel unsafe?
- How has unforgiveness or pride kept me from the relationships or peace I desire?
- Am I willing to give others the same mercy God gave me even when I didn't deserve it?
- What would my life look like if I truly lived free from bitterness and resentment?

CHAPTER 7: The Power of Surrender

"Trust in the Lord with all your heart and lean not on your own understanding."

– Proverbs 3:5

Introduction: You Can't Heal and Control Everything

Let's be real, especially for the men reading this: Most of us have been taught to trust no one, rely on ourselves, and control every outcome. Why? Because life taught us early: People disappoint. Plans fall apart. Pain is inevitable.

So we hold on tight. We calculate every move. We protect our emotions and play it safe. But Proverbs 3:5 tells us straight: "Trust in the Lord with ALL your heart..." That means let go. That means you're not in control, and you don't have to be.

Because the truth is: your understanding is limited. But God's vision is eternal.

This is one of the most quoted scriptures in the Bible, but it's also one of the hardest to live out, especially for men who have had to survive by depending on themselves for years. This chapter will teach you why true healing, breakthrough, and purpose can only come when you stop trusting your own limited view and start trusting the God who sees it all.

The need to control everything comes from a place of deep fear. Fear that if you let go, everything will fall apart. Fear that if you don't manage every detail, chaos will ensue. Fear that if you trust someone else, even God, you'll be disappointed again. But this fear is rooted in trauma, not truth. It's based on past pain, not present reality.

Most men develop a control addiction early in life as a survival mechanism. Maybe your parents were unreliable, so you learned to depend only on yourself. Maybe you were hurt by people you trusted, so you decided never to be vulnerable again. Maybe you experienced chaos in your childhood, so you became obsessed with creating order in your adult life.

But what started as a survival mechanism has become a prison. What began as protection has become a problem.

What felt like strength has become weakness. Because when you try to control everything, you actually control nothing. When you trust only yourself, you limit yourself to your own limited perspective, wisdom, and power.

Why This Scripture Is a Lifeline, Not Just a Command

You're not being asked to trust because God needs reassurance. You're being asked to trust because you need relief. Trying to figure everything out on your own will exhaust your mind, strain your relationships, steal your peace, and delay your healing.

The enemy wants you stuck in your own thoughts, second-guessing everything, doubting everyone, especially God. Because as long as you're leaning on your own understanding, you're leaning away from the very power that can actually change things. God is saying: "You don't need to know how, you just need to know Me."

Think about it: Every time you've tried to control a situation, how did it turn out? Every time you've attempted to manipulate an outcome, did you get the result you wanted? Every time you've refused to trust and insisted on handling everything yourself, did it bring you peace?

Most likely, your attempts at control have brought more stress, not less. More anxiety, not peace. More frustration, not fulfillment. Because control is an illusion. You can't control other people's choices. You can't control circumstances beyond your influence. You can't control the future, no matter how much you plan or prepare.

But here's what you can do: You can control your response to what you can't control. You can choose to trust God with what's beyond your power. You can decide to lean on His understanding when yours falls short. You can surrender your need to figure everything out and rest in the truth that He already has.

This isn't just about making life easier, though it will. This isn't just about reducing stress, though it does. This is about positioning yourself to receive what God wants to give you. Because God can't steer a parked car. He can't direct someone who's determined to go their own way. And He can't bless someone who believes they must earn everything through their own effort.

Trust Isn't Weak It's Spiritual Strength

Let's redefine what strength really looks like.

Strength isn't pretending you're never scared. Strength is saying, "God, I don't have the answers, but I trust You do."

When you trust God with all your heart, it means this:

- You trust Him when things are unclear.
- You trust Him when it's painful.
- You trust Him when the plan changes.
- You trust Him even when the storm doesn't stop, because you know who's in the boat with you.

The world has taught us that trust is weakness, that vulnerability is dangerous, that depending on anyone, even God, is risky. But that's backwards thinking.

Real strength is knowing your limitations and trusting Someone who has none.

Real power is understanding your finite perspective and leaning on Someone with infinite wisdom.

Real courage is letting go of what you can't control and holding onto what you can, your faith.

Trust takes more courage than control. Control feels safe because it gives the illusion that you're managing your life. But trust requires admitting that you don't have all the answers, that you need help, that you're not sufficient on your own. And for men conditioned to be self-sufficient, that can feel terrifying.

But here's what happens when you choose trust over control:

You discover that God is more reliable than your own efforts. You find that His plans are better than your plans. You learn that His timing is more perfect than your timing. You experience peace, not from having everything figured out, but from knowing that Someone else does.

Trust doesn't eliminate challenges, it changes how you face them.

Trust doesn't prevent problems, it transforms your perspective on them.

Trust doesn't guarantee everything will go your way, it guarantees that all things will work together for your good, if you love God and are called according to His purpose.

Why You Can't Lean on Your Own Understanding

Because your understanding is shaped by trauma, betrayal, insecurity, fear, ego, and a limited perspective, what feels like "logic" might actually be your trauma trying to protect you.

You might avoid love because you were once hurt, hold back vulnerability because you were abandoned, or strive to earn everything because no one ever gave you grace. But relying on your own understanding won't lead to peace, only pressure.

God says: "I'm not asking you to understand. I'm asking you to trust."

Your understanding is filtered through your experiences your wounds, your fears, and your limitations. If you've been betrayed, it tells you not to trust anyone. If you've been abandoned, it urges you to keep people at a distance. If you've been hurt, it convinces you to protect yourself at all costs.

But God's understanding isn't limited by your experiences. His wisdom isn't tainted by trauma. His perspective isn't clouded by pain. His plans aren't confined by your past. He sees the beginning from the end. He knows what you need before you even ask. He understands what's best for you, even when you don't.

When you lean on your own understanding, you're essentially saying, "God, my perspective is better than Yours. My wisdom is more reliable than Yours. My plans are superior to Yours." That's not just foolish, it's prideful. And it's exhausting.

Think about how much mental energy you spend trying to figure everything out. How much emotional energy you waste worrying about things beyond your control. How much physical energy you drain from the stress of trying to manage outcomes you can't influence.

Now imagine what could happen if you redirected all that energy into trusting God instead of trying to control everything. Imagine the peace you'd experience if you truly believed that He has your best interests at heart. Imagine the rest you'd find if you genuinely trusted that He's working all things together for your good.

The Trap of Overthinking

One of the ways we lean on our own understanding is by overthinking. We analyze every situation to exhaustion. We replay conversations, searching for hidden meanings. We worry about scenarios that may never unfold. We try to predict every possible outcome and prepare for every potential problem.

But overthinking isn't wisdom, it's worry. It's not preparation, it's paralysis. It's not responsibility, it's anxiety. And it keeps you stuck in your head instead of moving forward in faith.

Overthinking is simply delayed obedience. God gives you direction, but instead of acting on it, you dissect it. He offers clarity, but instead of progressing, you second-guess it. He opens doors, but instead of stepping through, you question whether they're the right ones.

Yet God doesn't call you to understand everything, He calls you to trust Him with everything. He doesn't require you to see the whole staircase, just to take the next step. He doesn't expect you to grasp His entire plan, only to follow His present direction.

When you overthink, you're essentially saying that your analysis carries more weight than God's instruction. You're placing your understanding above His guidance. You're trusting your mental processing more than His divine leading. But that's not faith, it's fear dressed up as wisdom.

Applying This Scripture in Real Life

Here's how you start walking this out, day by day:

Pray Before You Move

Before making your next decision, pause and ask:

"God, what would You have me do?"

This isn't about waiting for a voice from heaven or expecting a burning bush. It's about acknowledging God in your decisions and seeking His wisdom before you act.

Most men make choices based on what seems logical, feels safe, or appears most beneficial. But praying before you move means inviting God into the decision-making process. It's an admission that His wisdom surpasses yours and a posture of humility, allowing divine guidance to take the lead over human reasoning.

This doesn't mean becoming passive or neglecting the mind God has given you. It means surrendering your thoughts to His truth, your plans to His purpose, and your will to His way. It's about being open to direction that may not make sense to you, but makes perfect sense to Him.

Let Go of the Illusion of Control

Stop trying to predict or manipulate every outcome. Trust that if God allowed it, He's using it, even the pain. This is often the hardest part for most men because we've been conditioned to believe we're responsible for controlling our environment, our circumstances, and our outcomes.

But control is largely an illusion. You can influence some things, but you can't control most. You can make wise decisions, but you can't guarantee the results. You can work hard, but you can't ensure success. You can love people deeply, but you can't force them to love you back.

Letting go of control doesn't mean becoming irresponsible or passive. It means doing your part and trusting God with the outcome. It means making thoughtful choices and leaving the consequences to Him. It means giving your best effort and resting in His sovereignty.

When you try to control everything, you're essentially playing God. You're assuming responsibility that was never yours to carry. You're taking on burdens that were never meant for you. And that's not just exhausting, it's impossible.

Trade Worry for Worship

The moment you feel overwhelmed, worship. Speak God's name out loud. Remind yourself: He's got me. Even now.

Worry is simply meditation on the wrong thing. It's focusing on problems instead of solutions, on fear instead of faith, on what could go wrong instead of what God can make right.

But worship shifts your focus. It reminds you of God's character, His power, His faithfulness, His love. It moves your attention from your circumstances to your Savior, from your problems to your Provider, from your limitations to His limitless resources.

Worship isn't just about singing songs or attending church, though those are meaningful acts. Worship is acknowledging God's greatness in the middle of your struggles. It's declaring His faithfulness even when you can't see it. It's praising His goodness even when life feels anything but good.

When you choose to worship in the midst of worry, you're choosing faith over fear. You're trusting instead of panicking. You're standing on God's truth, not bowing to your temporary circumstances.

Stop Overthinking Everything

Overthinking is simply delayed obedience. You don't need 100% clarity, just enough faith to take the next step. God rarely reveals the full picture upfront. Instead, He gives you just enough light for the step ahead, just enough direction for the immediate decision, and just enough clarity for the current choice.

And that's intentional. If God showed you everything at once, there would be no need for faith. If He unveiled the entire plan from the beginning, you wouldn't have to trust Him daily. If He gave you all the answers immediately, you wouldn't need to depend on Him continually.

Faith means taking the next step even when the whole staircase isn't visible. It's about moving forward even when the destination is unclear. It's about obeying, even when the complete plan doesn't make sense.

When You Trust God, You Rest Differently

You don't panic the same way. You don't need all the answers. You don't have to prove yourself. You stop fighting battles that were never yours to fight in the first place, because when God is in charge, your job is obedience, not control.

When you truly trust God, it transforms the way you approach life. You sleep better because you're no longer lying awake trying to solve problems only He can fix. You relate better because you're not trying to manage other people's choices. You work better because you're no longer carrying the burden of outcomes that aren't your responsibility.

You parent differently when you trust God with your children's futures. You love differently when you trust Him with your relationships. You work differently when you trust Him with your career. You dream differently when you trust Him with your purpose.

Trust gives you permission to be human. It frees you from the pressure to be perfect, to have every answer, or to control every outcome. It allows you to do your best and leave the rest to God. It enables you to work diligently and rest peacefully, to plan wisely and trust deeply, to be both responsible and at peace.

The Freedom of Surrender

Surrendering control isn't losing, it's winning. It's not giving up, it's stepping into your true identity as a son of God who fully trusts his Father. It's not weakness, it's the greatest strength you can display.

When you surrender control to God, you're acknowledging that He is far better at being God than you are. You're recognizing that His ways are higher than yours, His thoughts greater than your thoughts. You're confessing that His love for you surpasses your own ability to care for yourself.

This surrender doesn't happen just once, it's a daily decision. Each morning, you must choose again to trust God instead of relying on yourself. Every time a crisis arises, you're faced with the choice to lean on His understanding rather than your own. Whenever fear tempts you to take back control, you must once again choose to let God lead.

But the more you practice surrender, the more natural it becomes. The more you experience God's faithfulness when you trust Him, the easier it gets to trust Him again. And the more you witness His wisdom in moments where you couldn't see the way forward, the more willing you become to follow His lead.

Closing Declaration

I release my need to understand everything. I choose to trust the God who sees all, knows all, and loves me unconditionally. I will not lean on fear, ego, or pain, I will lean on truth. I will lean on Him.

Brother, it's time to let go of the wheel. It's time to stop trying to drive your life from the passenger seat. It's time to trust that the God who created you knows how to direct you, the God who saved you knows how to sustain you, and the God who called you knows how to complete what He started in you.

Your understanding is limited, but His is limitless. Your perspective is finite, but His is eternal. Your wisdom is flawed, but His is perfect. Your strength is inadequate, but His is more than enough.

Trust in the Lord with all your heart, not just the parts you feel safe giving Him, but all of it: your fears, your hopes, your plans, your dreams, your relationships, your future, all of it.

Love Them More Than Your Demons

He's got you. Even now. Especially now.

Prayer

Father, I confess that I've been trying to control what only You can control.

I've been leaning on my own understanding instead of trusting in Your wisdom.

I've been carrying burdens that were never mine to bear and trying to solve problems that only You can solve.

Today I choose to let go. I choose to trust You with all my heart, not just the parts

I feel safe giving You.

Help me to stop overthinking and start obeying. Help me to stop worrying and start worshipping.

Help me to stop trying to figure everything out and start following Your lead.

I trust that Your plans for me are good, that Your timing is perfect, and that Your love never fails.

In Jesus' name,

Amen.

William "King" Hollis

Reflection Questions

- What area of my life am I still trying to control instead of trusting God with?
- What "understanding" have I been leaning on that may actually be rooted in fear or trauma?
- What would it look like to trust God with all my heart not just the parts I feel safe giving Him?
- When was the last time I truly surrendered something and let God handle it?
- How would my life change if I truly believed that God's plans for me are good and His timing is perfect?

CHAPTER 8: Walking Through the Fire

"When you walk through the fire, you shall not be burned, nor shall the flame scorch you."

– Isaiah 43:2

Introduction: The Fire Is Real, But So Is the Promise

Let's not sugarcoat it, some days feel like hell. Some seasons feel like you're being ripped apart from the inside out. You've cried alone at night with no one to wipe your tears. You've smiled in public while breaking in private. You've walked through fires that should've destroyed you.

But look at you. Still standing. Still breathing. Still fighting. That's not a coincidence, that's a covenant.

God said, "When you walk through the fire…" not if, not maybe, not once or twice. You will walk through fire. But here's the promise: "You shall not be burned; the flame shall not scorch you."

This scripture is a survival promise, not just poetic, but prophetic. It reminds you that even when life turns up the heat, God doesn't always remove the fire, He walks with you through it. This chapter will show you why it's crucial to apply this verse, and how embracing it can anchor you through depression, betrayal, loss, and spiritual warfare.

Every man reading this has walked through some kind of fire. Maybe it was the fire of abandonment when your father left. Maybe it was the fire of betrayal when someone you trusted broke your heart. Maybe it was the fire of failure when your dreams came crashing down. Maybe it was the fire of addiction when you thought you'd never get clean. Or maybe it was the fire of depression, when you couldn't see a way out of the darkness.

But here you are. Still reading. Still breathing. Still hoping for something better. That's not an accident. That's not just luck. That's not just good genes or strong willpower. That's the hand of God, protecting you in the fire, sustaining you through the flames, keeping you from being consumed by what should have destroyed you.

Why This Verse Matters Right Now

This scripture isn't just a nice phrase to memorize, it's a mindset to live by. Because the fire will come: The divorce will hurt. The loss will leave a mark. The betrayal will sting. The depression will drain you. The addiction will whisper again.

But this verse reminds you, the fire doesn't get the final word. God does. And when you apply that truth, it changes how you walk through pain. You stop asking, "Why me?" and start declaring, "Even this won't destroy me."

Most men do everything they can to avoid the fire. We design our lives to minimize pain, disappointment, and difficulty. We build walls to protect ourselves from getting hurt. We make decisions based on what feels safest, not on what God is calling us to do. But Isaiah 43:2 makes it clear, fire is inevitable. The real question isn't whether you'll face the fire; it's whether you'll walk through it with faith or fear.

The enemy wants you to believe the fire proves God has left you. He wants you to think struggle means you're outside of God's will. He wants you to assume pain means God doesn't love you. But that's not what this verse teaches.

It teaches that God expects you to walk through the fire, but He promises to walk through it with you.

When you understand that truth, everything shifts. You stop being surprised by trials and start being prepared for them. You stop feeling like a victim of your circumstances and start seeing yourself as a victor through them. You stop running from the fire and start walking through it, with confidence.

What the Fire Teaches You

You Learn That Pain Doesn't Define You Just because you're in the fire doesn't mean you've failed. It means God is refining something in you that can't be built in comfort. Fire has a way of burning away what's unnecessary and strengthening what truly matters. The heat reveals what's real and what's fake, what's lasting and what's fleeting, what's valuable and what's worthless.

When gold is refined, it's placed in intense heat that burns away impurities, leaving behind pure, precious metal. The fire doesn't destroy the gold, it purifies it. The heat doesn't lessen its worth, it increases it. The flames don't weaken it, they make it stronger.

That's exactly what God is doing in your life through the fire. He's burning away pride, selfishness, fear, and anything else holding you back from becoming the man He created you to be. He's building your faith, refining your character, and deepening your dependence on Him. He's purifying your motives, your heart, and your relationships, with Him and with others.

The fire isn't punishment, it's preparation. It's not a sign of God being cruel, it's a sign of His kindness. It's not evidence of His absence, it's proof of His presence. Because God never wastes pain. He uses every trial, every struggle, and every difficult season to shape you into the man He's called you to be.

You Learn What You're Really Made Of

Some of your strongest qualities, resilience, patience, and faith, are revealed only in the furnace. Comfort doesn't build character. Easy times don't develop endurance. Smooth sailing doesn't strengthen spiritual muscles. It's in the fire that you discover what you're truly made of.

Think about the strongest people you know. Not those who've had easy lives, but those who've walked through hell and come out better, not bitter. The ones who faced impossible odds and refused to give up. The ones who walked through fire and came out refined, not ruined.

What made them strong wasn't the absence of struggle, it was the presence of God in the struggle. What built their character wasn't escaping pain, it was trusting God through it. What grew their faith wasn't having all the answers, it was believing God when nothing made sense.

You carry a strength you haven't even tapped into yet. A faith waiting to be awakened. A resilience that rises only when it's most needed. But you'll never know what you're truly made of until you're tested by fire.

You Learn Who God Really Is

He's not a distant judge, He's the God who steps into the fire with you. Just as He did with the three Hebrew boys in Daniel 3, they didn't walk alone, and neither do you.

When Shadrach, Meshach, and Abednego were thrown into the fiery furnace, King Nebuchadnezzar expected to see three men burning. But instead, he saw four men walking unharmed in the fire. The fourth man, he said, looked like "a son of the gods." That fourth man was Jesus, walking with them in their darkest hour.

The same Jesus who walked with them in the fire is walking with you in yours. He's not watching from a distance, hoping you make it through. He's not cheering from the sidelines, simply wishing you well. He's in the fire with you, protecting you, sustaining you, and keeping you from being consumed.

This is who God truly is, not a distant deity who watches your pain from afar, but a loving Father who steps into it with you. Not a God who sends fire to punish, but one who walks with you through the fire to refine you. Not a God who turns away in hardship, but one who comes even closer in it.

Why You Must Implement This Scripture

Because if you don't, you'll mistake the fire for punishment, instead of preparation. If you don't apply this truth, you'll let trauma define you, let pain harden you, let loss steal your belief in love, and let one bad chapter convince you the whole story is over.

But when you apply Isaiah 43:2, you remember: "This fire is real, but so is my God. I may feel the heat, but I will not be destroyed."

Application means more than just knowing the verse, it means living it. It means bringing this truth into your specific situation, your current struggle, your present fire. It means clinging to this promise as your anchor when life's storms threaten to pull you under.

Without application, this verse is just information. With application, it becomes transformation. Without implementation, it's just words on a page. With implementation, it becomes power in your life.

Most men struggle with application because it asks something unnatural: to trust God in the middle of pain rather than escape it. It asks them to walk through the fire, not around it. It asks them to believe God's promise even when circumstances seem to contradict it.

But application is what separates men who merely survive their trials from men who are strengthened by them. Application distinguishes those who simply endure hardship from those who are transformed by it. It's what turns a man from a victim of his circumstances into a victor through them.

What Does It Look Like to Walk Through Fire Without Being Burned?

It means you're honest about your pain, but you're not defined by it. You cry, but you don't give up. You walk slowly, but you keep moving forward. You don't stop praising just because the pressure has increased.

Walking through fire without being burned doesn't mean you don't feel the heat. It doesn't mean you're untouched by the flames. It doesn't mean you pretend everything is okay when it isn't. It means you acknowledge the fire while trusting the Promise Keeper.

It means you carry the full weight of your circumstances while standing on the unshakable foundation of God's Word. It means you face the reality of your pain while resting in the certainty of God's protection. It means you wrestle with your questions while holding tightly to your faith.

Walking through fire without being burned looks like David writing psalms while fleeing from Saul. It looks like Job worshipping while losing everything. It looks like Paul singing in prison while facing execution. It looks like Jesus praying in the garden while walking toward the cross.

It's not the absence of struggle, it's the presence of faith in the midst of it. It's not the elimination of pain, it's the application of truth in the middle of the pain. It's not avoiding the fire, it's the assurance of God's presence within it.

How to Live This Daily

Speak It Over Yourself in Dark Seasons

Say it out loud: "I'm walking through fire, but I will not be burned." Remind your spirit who's really in charge, not the storm, not the sickness, not the situation, but God.

Words carry power, especially the words you speak over yourself. When you declare God's truth over your circumstances, you're not just making noise, you're making war. You're fighting against discouragement, despair, and defeat with the weapon of God's Word.

Speaking truth over yourself in dark seasons isn't about positive thinking, it's a prophetic declaration. You're not pretending everything is fine when it isn't; you're reminding yourself of what God has promised, even when there's no visible sign of that promise.

This daily declaration becomes an anchor for your soul when everything else feels unstable. It becomes a lifeline when you feel like you're drowning. It becomes a light when you can't see the way forward.

Look at Your Scars as Proof, Not Shame

Your scars don't mean you lost, they mean you survived. They are proof that the fire didn't win. Each scar tells a story of God's protection. Every healed wound is a testimony of His power. Every battle you endured is evidence that you are more than a conqueror.

Many men view their scars as signs of failure, weakness, or defeat. But God sees them as marks of survival, strength, and victory. Your scars are proof that you walked through fire, and lived to tell the story. They show that what was meant to destroy you actually made you stronger.

Stop hiding your scars, start celebrating them. Stop being ashamed of your story, start sharing your testimony. Don't see your past pain as a disqualification. See it as your qualification to help others walking through similar fires.

Stay Close to God in the Heat

Don't run from Him, run to Him. The fire becomes bearable when you're walking with the One who controls the flames. When the heat intensifies, that's exactly when you need to draw closer to God, not pull away. When the pressure increases, that's when you must lean harder on His promises, not abandon them.

Many men make the mistake of distancing themselves from God when life gets hard. They believe that if God truly loved them, He wouldn't allow them to suffer. They assume that if God really had a plan for their lives, that plan wouldn't involve pain. But that's not biblical thinking.

Scripture is filled with stories of people who walked closely with God and still faced the fire. Noah walked with God, and still endured the flood. Abraham walked with God, and still experienced delays and disappointments. Moses walked with God, and still encountered opposition and obstacles. David walked with God, and still stood against enemies and adversity.

The difference wasn't that they avoided the fire, it's that they faced it with God. They didn't walk around the flames; they walked through them with the One who created and controls the fire.

The Purpose of Fire

Fire isn't random, it's purposeful. God doesn't allow fire in your life to destroy you; He allows it to develop you. He doesn't permit trials to break you; He permits them to build you. He doesn't send struggles to defeat you; He sends them to refine you.

Fire serves multiple purposes in the life of a believer. It burns away the impurities that hinder your growth. It strengthens the faith that might otherwise remain weak. It develops the kind of character that can only be forged through difficulty. It builds endurance that prepares you for greater assignments. It deepens your dependence on God and increases your appreciation for His grace.

Fire also serves as a testimony to others. When people see you walking through fire without being consumed, they want to know your secret. When they see you maintaining faith in the middle of hardship, they're drawn to the source of that faith. When they witness your peace in the storm, they become curious about the foundation of that peace.

Your fire becomes a platform for God's glory when you walk through it with faith instead of fear. Your trial becomes a testimony when you trust God's promises rather than your circumstances. Your struggle becomes your strength when you lean on God's grace instead of your own understanding.

The Promise of Protection

Isaiah 43:2 doesn't promise that you won't face the fire, it promises the fire won't consume you. It doesn't guarantee you won't feel the heat, it guarantees the heat won't destroy you. It doesn't say you'll avoid hardship, it says you'll overcome it.

This promise isn't based on your strength, it's grounded in God's faithfulness. It's not about your ability to withstand the fire, it's about God's power to protect you in it. It doesn't depend on flawless faith, it depends on God's unchanging love.

When you truly grasp this promise, it reshapes how you face every trial. You don't walk into the fire wondering if you'll make it, you walk in confident that you'll come out stronger. You don't face hardship questioning God's love, you face it resting in His protection. You don't endure pain doubting God's plan, you endure it trusting in His purpose.

Living as a Fire Walker

When you truly understand and embrace Isaiah 43:2, you become what I call a fire walker, not someone who avoids hardship, but someone who walks through it with unwavering confidence. You become a person who doesn't fear trials but confronts them with faith. You don't run from pain, you move through it with purpose.

Fire walkers don't search for easy roads, they trust God on the difficult ones. They don't crave comfort, they pursue meaning. They don't ask for trials to be taken away, they pray for strength to endure them and for wisdom to grow through them.

Fire walkers become beacons of encouragement to others going through the fire. They become living testimonies of God's faithfulness. They stand as proof that it's possible to walk through hell and come out whole, to face fire and not be consumed, to endure pain and still lift up praise.

Closing Declaration

The fire will not consume me. The flames will not define me.

I walk through pain, but I walk with purpose.

God is with me in the fire, and that means I cannot be destroyed.

I am not broken beyond repair. I am battle-tested. I am chosen. I am still here, and that's the proof.

Brother, look at your life. Look at what you've survived. Look at the fires you've walked through. Look at the flames that should have consumed you, but didn't.

That's not an accident, that's God's protection. That's not luck, That's God's love. That's not a coincidence, That's covenant.

You're still here. That's the proof. That's the evidence. That's the testimony.

You've been through fire before, and survived. You'll go through fire again, and you'll survive.

Prayer

Father, thank You that You don't promise to keep me from fire, but You promise to keep me safe in fire.

Thank You that when I walk through flames, I don't walk alone.

Help me to see my current trials not as punishment but as preparation, not as evidence of

Your absence is but proof of Your presence.

Give me the faith to trust Your promise when my circumstances seem to contradict it.

Help me to speak Your truth over my situation even when my emotions want to declare defeat.

Turn my scars into testimonies, my trials into triumphs, and my pain into purpose. I believe that this fire will not consume me because

You are with me in it.

In Jesus' name,

Amen.

William "King" Hollis

Reflection Questions

- What fire have I been through that should've taken me out but didn't?
- Am I allowing my current fire to shape me or shut me down?
- How can I remind myself daily that God is walking with me through the flames?
- What scar in my life can I start seeing as proof of God's protection instead of pain?
- How can I use my experience of surviving fire to encourage others who are currently facing flames?

CHAPTER 9: You Can't Heal Alone

"As iron sharpens iron, so one person sharpens another."

– Proverbs 27:17

Introduction: You Need Real Brothers

If the enemy can isolate you, he can destroy you. And let's be honest, many men suffer in silence. We've been trained to keep it to ourselves: don't talk about it, don't cry about it, don't let them see you weak.

But Proverbs 27:17 breaks that mindset wide open: "As iron sharpens iron, so one person sharpens another."

That means you can't sharpen yourself. You need people who don't just agree with you, they challenge you, refine you, and build you up.

This scripture speaks to one of the most essential, yet often overlooked, areas in a man's healing journey: his relationships with other men. In a world that encourages isolation, pride, and silent suffering, this verse reminds us: you were never meant to do life alone.

The enemy has convinced most men that needing others is weakness, that asking for help is failure, and that vulnerability is dangerous. He's sold us the lie that real men handle everything themselves, that true strength means never needing anyone, that independence is more valuable than interdependence.

But that's not God's design. That's not biblical masculinity. That's not how healing happens. God created you for community, designed you for relationship, and called you to grow in the context of authentic brotherhood.

Why You Can't Heal in Isolation

The enemy doesn't mind if you read this book, as long as you never apply it with real people. Healing becomes powerful when it becomes relational.

You can pray in private, but you're sharpened in community. You can possess wisdom, but accountability comes through brotherhood. You can quote scripture, but you grow when someone holds you to it. You were never meant to do this alone.

Isolation is one of the enemy's most effective strategies because it cuts you off from the very relationships God intends to use for your growth. When you're isolated, you become vulnerable to deception, because no one is there to challenge your thinking. You become susceptible to discouragement, because no one is there to encourage you. You become prone to giving up, because no one is there to help you keep going.

But isolation isn't always something the enemy forces on you, it's often something you choose. You choose it because you're afraid of being hurt again. You choose it because you don't want anyone to see your struggles. You choose it because you've been conditioned to believe that needing others is weakness.

The truth is, isolation feels safer than vulnerability. It feels easier than risking rejection. It feels more comfortable than facing judgment. But isolation doesn't heal, it hardens. It doesn't strengthen, it weakens. It doesn't protect, it imprisons.

God never intended for you to heal in a vacuum. He designed healing to happen in the context of relationship, relationship with Him and relationship with others. When you try to heal alone, you work against God's design for your life.

What "Iron Sharpens Iron" Really Means

This verse isn't just about friendship, it's about friction. Iron doesn't sharpen iron without pressure, grinding, and sometimes heat.

That's what godly relationships do: they check you when you're slipping, pray with you when you're weak, and refuse to let you settle for less than God's best. They remind you of who you are when you forget.

But here's the truth: sharpening only happens when you're willing to be confronted. You've got to drop the ego, stop hiding behind surface-level conversations, and get real.

The process of iron sharpening iron isn't gentle, it's intentional friction that creates a sharper edge. When two pieces of iron rub against each other, sparks fly, heat is generated, and rough edges are smoothed out. The result is a more effective, sharper tool.

The same is true in relationships. When godly men invest in each other's lives, friction is inevitable. There will be uncomfortable conversations. Moments when your pride is challenged, your blind spots exposed, and your weaknesses brought to light. But that friction isn't meant to harm you, it's meant to help you.

Most men avoid this kind of friction because it's uncomfortable. They prefer relationships that are easy, non-confrontational, and comfortable. They surround themselves with people who always agree with them, always encourage them, and never challenge them. But those aren't sharpening relationships, they're flattering ones.

Flattering relationships make you feel good in the moment, but they don't help you grow over time. They affirm who you are now but don't push you to become who God called you to be. They comfort your flesh but do nothing to strengthen your spirit.

Sharpening relationships are different. They love you too much to leave you where you are. They see your potential and refuse to let you settle. They speak truth even when it's hard to hear. They hold you accountable even when it's uncomfortable. They challenge you to grow, even when growth demands change.

Why You Must Implement This Scripture

If you don't apply Proverbs 27:17, you'll keep trusting no one, repeating the same cycles, believing unchecked lies, and carrying burdens alone, burdens that were never meant to be yours alone. You'll end up in rooms full of people, yet still feel unseen and unsharpened.

This verse is about more than friendship, it's about spiritual survival. You weren't created to be a dull blade. You were made to cut through generational curses, stand in truth, and lead with power, but you need the right people to sharpen you.

Without living out this scripture, you'll remain stuck in patterns that leave you defeated. You'll keep making the same mistakes because there's no one to help you recognize your blind spots. You'll go on believing lies because there's no one to speak truth into your life. You'll continue bearing burdens alone that were always meant to be shared.

Applying this verse means more than simply having friends, it means having the right kind of friends. It means surrounding yourself with people committed to your growth, not just your comfort. It's about building relationships that challenge you to grow, not just ones that make you feel good.

The enemy thrives on isolation because isolated men are easier to defeat. When you're alone, you're more vulnerable to temptation. When you're isolated, you're more susceptible to deception. And when you're by yourself, you're more likely to give up when things get hard.

But when you're in authentic community with other godly men, you gain support when you're struggling, accountability when you're slipping, and encouragement when you're discouraged. You have people who will fight for you when you lack the strength to fight for yourself. You have brothers who remind you of who you are, especially when you forget.

What Real Sharpening Relationships Look Like

They aren't built on popularity, business connections, or flattery.

They are grounded in accountability, shared faith, honest conversations, mutual respect, and growth in God.

Seek out people who won't let you lie to yourself, who refuse to celebrate your dysfunction, who speak both life and correction, and who point you to Christ, not just to comfort.

Genuine sharpening relationships are defined by several key elements:

Mutual commitment to growth. Both individuals are committed to becoming better versions of themselves.

They're not content to remain as they are, they desire growth spiritually, emotionally, and relationally.

They view the relationship as an opportunity to help one another become the men God has called them to be.

Honest communication. There's no pretending in sharpening relationships.

Both individuals are honest about their struggles, weaknesses, and failures.

They cultivate safe spaces where vulnerability is welcomed, not judged.

They speak the truth, even when it's hard to hear or difficult to say.

Shared values. Sharpening relationships are built on a foundation of shared beliefs and values.

Both individuals are committed to following Christ, living by biblical principles, and pursuing God's will for their lives.

This shared foundation fosters unity and provides clear direction for the relationship.

Accountability. Both individuals give each other permission to ask hard questions, challenge destructive behaviors, and call out blind spots.

They don't just celebrate one another's successes, they also address each other's failures.

They love each other too much to let harmful patterns continue unchecked.

Intentionality. These relationships don't happen by accident, they're intentionally cultivated.

Both individuals invest time, energy, and effort into building the connection.

They prioritize quality time, meaningful conversations, and mutual support through difficult seasons.

Confidentiality. What's shared within the relationship stays within the relationship.

Both individuals trust that their vulnerabilities, struggles, and failures won't be used against them or disclosed to others.

This builds a safe space for genuine connection and personal growth.

The Cost of Isolation

Isolation always costs more than it protects. When you choose to go through life alone, you pay a price far greater than the risk of relationship.

You forfeit the benefit of other perspectives, the strength found in shared burdens, and the growth that comes through authentic community.

Isolated men often struggle with distorted thinking because no one is there to challenge their perspective.

They develop blind spots that remain unaddressed, simply because no one is present to point them out.

They make poor decisions due to the absence of wise counsel. They repeat destructive patterns because no one helps them recognize the cycle.

Isolation also makes you more vulnerable to spiritual attack. The enemy knows that a man standing alone is easier to defeat than one standing in fellowship.

When you're isolated, you lack the prayer support, encouragement, and accountability that help you resist temptation and overcome life's challenges.

But perhaps the greatest cost of isolation is missing the opportunity to experience the fullness of what God intends for your life.

God designed you to live in community, to be known and loved by others, to contribute to their growth while being sharpened by their investment in you.

When you choose isolation, you miss out on the joy of deep friendship, the strength of mutual support, and the transformation that happens when iron sharpens iron.

You end up living beneath the level of God's intention for your life.

Don't Mistake Loneliness for Strength

Some of the strongest-looking men are also the loneliest. You might be surrounded, but not sharpened. Admired, but not covered.

Brother, stop confusing strength with silence. Even Jesus had twelve. Even Jesus needed community.

Many men mistake loneliness for strength because they've been taught that needing others is weakness.

They believe handling everything alone is a mark of maturity and power.

But that's not biblical thinking, it's cultural conditioning, and it runs contrary to God's design.

Jesus, the strongest man who ever lived, didn't do ministry alone.

He chose twelve disciples to walk with Him, learn from Him, and support Him in His mission.

He invested deeply in relationships with men like Peter, James, and John.

He welcomed the support of friends like Mary, Martha, and Lazarus.

Even Jesus, though fully God, chose to live and minister in community.

If Jesus needed community, what makes you think you don't?

If the Son of God valued relationships and invested in friendships, why do you believe you can succeed alone?

If the strongest man in history surrounded Himself with others, why are you trying to live in isolation?

The truth is, real strength is knowing when you need help, and being willing to ask for it.

Real maturity means recognizing you were created for relationship and choosing to invest in authentic community.

And real courage? It's being vulnerable enough to share your struggles, and strong enough to help others with theirs.

How to Start Living This Out

Ask God to Send the Right People Pray specifically: "Lord, send me men who will sharpen me, not flatter me."

Don't just pray for friends, pray for iron. Don't just ask for companions, ask for challengers.

Don't just seek people who make you feel good, seek people who help you grow.

This prayer takes faith, because God might send people who don't match your natural preferences.

He might connect you with men who are different from you, who challenge your thinking, and who push you out of your comfort zone.

But that's exactly what growth demands. Be intentional in your prayer. Ask God for men who love Him more than they love your approval.

Ask for brothers who care more about your character than your comfort.

Ask for friends who will speak the truth even when it's hard to hear.

Be Willing to Go First

Open up. Be honest. You might be the one who breaks the wall for another man to find freedom.

Someone has to be willing to go first, to be vulnerable. Someone has to be brave enough to share their struggles. Someone has to create a safe space where other men feel permission to be real.

That someone might be you. You might be the one God uses to spark authentic relationships in your circle.

You might be the first in your group to admit you don't have it all together.

You might be the catalyst that transforms surface-level friendships into life-giving, life-changing connections.

Going first is scary because you don't know how others will respond.

They might judge you, reject you, or use your vulnerability against you.

But they might also feel relieved that someone finally gave them permission to be honest.

They might be grateful you created space for authenticity. They might follow your lead, and open up about their own struggles.

Stay Around the Fire

Find spaces, men's groups, Bible studies, brotherhood circles, where the standard is growth and truth, not just vibes and small talk.

Look for environments where men are committed to becoming better, not just feeling better.

Pursue communities where conversations go deeper than sports, work, and surface-level chatter.

These spaces don't always exist naturally, sometimes, you have to create them.

You may need to start a men's group at your church, organize regular meetups with like-minded men, or join an existing group that values spiritual growth and authentic connection.

The key is consistency. Don't just show up when it's convenient, make it a priority. Don't only participate when you feel like it, commit to the process.

Real sharpening takes place over time through steady investment in meaningful relationships.

Be Sharpened and Sharpen Others

Don't just look for someone to help you, be someone who helps others grow.

The best way to attract sharpening relationships is to become a sharpening person. The most effective way to find iron is to become iron yourself.

This means being willing to have hard conversations with other men when they need to hear the truth.

It means offering encouragement when they're discouraged and providing accountability when they're slipping.

It means investing in their growth even when there's no immediate benefit to you.

When you become the kind of friend you want to have, you attract the kind of friends you need.

When you demonstrate that you're a safe place for other people's vulnerabilities, they're more likely to be vulnerable with you.

When you show that you're committed to growth and accountability, others who value those things are drawn to build relationship with you.

The Process of Sharpening

Sharpening is a process, not a one-time event. It unfolds over time through consistent friction, honest conversation, and a mutual commitment to growth.

It demands patience, humility, and a willingness to endure temporary discomfort for long-term transformation.

The journey often begins with surface-level interaction and gradually deepens into greater authenticity and accountability.

It may start with casual conversation but grows into a life-changing relationship.

It begins by sharing successes and evolves into sharing struggles.

This process can't be rushed, but it can be intentionally cultivated.

You create an environment where sharpening occurs by being consistent, authentic, and committed to others' growth.

You accelerate the process by being willing to go deeper, ask harder questions, and confront difficult topics.

The Fruit of Sharpening Relationships

When you invest in iron-sharpening-iron relationships, you gain benefits that reach far beyond the relationships themselves.

You become a better man, a stronger leader, and a more effective husband and father.

You cultivate spiritual maturity, emotional intelligence, and relational skills that serve you in every area of life. You also become a source of strength and growth for others.

Your willingness to be sharpened makes you more effective at sharpening others.

Your commitment to growth inspires others to pursue it. Your authenticity gives others permission to be real.

The fruit of these relationships carries into future generations. When you model healthy masculine relationships for your sons, you teach them that real men don't suffer in silence.

When you demonstrate the value of accountability to younger men, you show them that true strength comes through communit not isolation.

Closing Declaration

"I will not walk alone. I will not suffer in silence. I will surround myself with men who sharpen me, stretch me, and push me closer to purpose. I am open. I am accountable. I am not just iron I am sharpened iron."

Brother, you were never meant to do this alone.

The healing you're seeking, the growth you're pursuing, the purpose you're chasing, all of it is designed to happen within the context of authentic relationships with other men on the same journey.

Stop buying into the lie that needing others is weakness. Stop believing that vulnerability is dangerous. Stop thinking you can heal, grow, and succeed in isolation.

You can't sharpen yourself any more than a knife can sharpen itself.

You need iron. You need friction. You need men who love you enough to challenge you.

Your healing depends on it. Your growth requires it. Your purpose demands it.

You can't heal alone, and you don't have to.

Prayer

Father, I confess that I've been trying to do life alone.

I've been hiding behind walls of pride, fear, and self-sufficiency.

I've been believing the lie that needing others is weakness when You designed me for community.

Send me men who will sharpen me, men who love You more than they love my approval, men who care more about my character than my comfort.

Give me the courage to be vulnerable, the wisdom to choose good friends, and the commitment to invest in relationships that help me grow.

Make me the kind of friend to others that I want them to be to me.

Help me to be iron that sharpens and iron that is willing to be sharpened.

In Jesus' name,

Amen

William "King" Hollis

Reflection Questions

- Who do I have in my life that sharpens me not just agrees with me?
- Am I open to correction, or do I avoid accountability?
- Have I been isolating out of pride, fear, or pain?
- What kind of friend or brother do I need to become for others?
- What walls have I built that prevent others from getting close enough to help me grow?

CHAPTER 10: Becoming Whole Again

"He heals the brokenhearted and binds up their wounds."

– Psalm 147:3

Introduction: What Happens When You Pretend You're Not Bleeding?

Too many men are walking around with open wounds they've learned to hide behind a smile, a hustle, a hard shell, or a sharp tongue. In today's world, especially for men, crying is seen as weakness. Vulnerability is dangerous. Talking about pain? That's not considered "manly."

So what do we do? We bleed quietly. We act strong while falling apart inside. We isolate instead of asking for help. We build walls instead of bridges. And most dangerously, we get used to being broken.

But Psalm 147:3 tells us the truth we've needed to hear all along:

"He heals the brokenhearted and binds up their wounds."

That means God doesn't ignore your pain, He enters it. He doesn't just patch it up, He heals it. But you've got to stop hiding it and let Him touch it.

This verse speaks to the heart of healing: God doesn't just observe brokenness, He steps into it. He heals. He binds. He restores what others tried to bury.

For every man who's carried pain in silence, who's bled emotionally while smiling publicly, this verse is a lifeline.

The tragedy of modern masculinity is that we've been taught to hide our wounds so well, we've forgotten they exist. We've become experts at compartmentalizing pain, professionals at pretending we're fine, masters at moving forward without dealing with what's behind us.

But unhealed wounds don't disappear, they fester. They infect every area of our lives. They influence our decisions, relationships, self-perception, and our ability to trust and love.

Why This Scripture Matters in Your Healing Journey

This verse isn't just comforting, it's instructional. It shows us three things:

God acknowledges your pain. He doesn't tell you to "man up" and move on.

He sees every crack, every tear, and every memory that still stings.

God specializes in heart work. He heals the brokenhearted, not just the wounded body, but the fractured soul.

God doesn't leave you exposed. He binds your wounds, meaning He tends to the areas that are still vulnerable, still tender, still bleeding.

You don't need to hide from God, you need to hand everything over to Him.

Many men struggle with this because we've been conditioned to view pain as something to conquer, not something to process. We've been taught that strength means pushing through instead of working through. We've been told that healing means forgetting, rather than integrating.

But God's approach to healing is different from the world's. The world says to ignore your pain, deny your wounds, and pretend nothing happened. God says to acknowledge your pain, confront your wounds, and allow Him to heal what's been broken.

The world treats symptoms; God addresses root causes. The world offers temporary relief; God provides lasting healing. The world places band-aids on deep wounds; God performs soul surgery.

This Scripture matters because it reveals God's heart toward the broken. He's not repelled by your brokenness, He's drawn to it. He's not frustrated by your healing process, He's fully invested in it. He's not shocked by the depth of your pain, He's committed to the depth of your healing.

Why You Must Implement This Scripture

If you don't implement this, you'll keep choosing numbness over healing, repeating toxic patterns inherited from unhealed pain, damaging relationships because of emotional wounds you never addressed, and wearing masks to protect your image while your identity suffers.

You weren't built to carry this pain alone. You weren't designed to heal through distraction. You were created to be whole, and that begins by letting God touch the broken places.

Applying this Scripture isn't optional, it's essential. Because unhealed wounds don't just affect you, they impact everyone around you. Your children absorb the weight of your unprocessed trauma. Your wife bears the burden of your unhealed hurt. Your friends encounter the walls you've built to protect your wounds.

When you refuse to let God heal what you won't talk about, you're not just hurting yourself, you're wounding the people you love most. You're passing down pain instead of healing. You're transferring trauma instead of transformation. You're modeling dysfunction instead of reflecting wholeness.

But when you apply this Scripture, when you let God heal the brokenhearted parts of you and bind up your wounds, you break cycles instead of continuing them. You model healing instead of hiding. You show that real men face their pain and allow God to transform it into purpose.

Implementation takes courage, the courage to admit you're broken, acknowledge your pain, ask for help, and trust God with your deepest wounds. It takes humility, the humility to admit you can't heal yourself, to recognize your need for divine intervention, and to surrender control of your healing process to God.

But implementation also brings freedom, freedom from the burden of carrying pain alone, freedom from the exhaustion of pretending you're fine, and freedom from the prison of unhealed wounds that keep you trapped in cycles of dysfunction.

Let God Be the Surgeon, Not Just the Savior

Many want God to bless them, few invite Him to break and reset what's out of alignment. But healing often feels worse before it feels better. Like a surgeon, God doesn't just numb the pain, He goes to the root of it.

He wants to heal the boy in you who was never affirmed, bind the soul of the man who's tired of pretending he's okay, and restore the father, the husband, the leader that life tried to silence. But you have to give Him access.

Most men are comfortable with God as Savior, the One who forgives their sins and secures their place in heaven. But they struggle with God as Surgeon, the One who cuts away infected tissue, removes toxic patterns, and operates on the deepest parts of their souls.

The Surgeon requires a different level of trust. When you go under the knife, you surrender all control. You trust that the Surgeon knows what He's doing, that the cutting is necessary, that the pain is purposeful, and that the result will be worth the process.

God wants to perform soul surgery on you, but He needs your consent. He won't force His way into your deepest wounds. He won't operate without your permission. He won't heal what you won't acknowledge, address what you won't confront, or restore what you won't surrender.

But when you give Him access, when you invite Him into your deepest pain, when you trust Him to heal what you can't fix, miraculous things happen. Wounds that have festered for years begin to heal. Patterns that have controlled your life begin to break. Lies that have defined your identity begin to dissolve.

The surgical process is not comfortable. God must cut away scar tissue that has shielded your wounds. He must remove infected thinking that has poisoned your perspective. He must reset bones that healed incorrectly the first time. But the temporary discomfort of divine surgery is worth the lasting freedom of divine healing.

Love Them More Than Your Demons

The Hidden Cost of Hidden Wounds

When you hide your wounds, you pay a price that reaches far beyond your own pain.

Hidden wounds lead to hidden dysfunction. Secret pain produces secret patterns. Unaddressed trauma gives rise to unconscious behaviors that sabotage your relationships, your opportunities, and your purpose.

Hidden wounds make you reactive instead of responsive. They cause you to interpret neutral situations through the lens of past pain. They make you defensive when you should be open, suspicious when you should trust, and angry when you should understand.

They also create emotional unavailability. When you're expending energy hiding your pain, you lack the emotional capacity to invest in others. When you're protecting your wounds, you can't offer your heart. When you're managing your image, you can't be authentic in your relationships.

Perhaps most tragically, hidden wounds rob you of the ministry that could grow from your mess. Your greatest pain could become your greatest platform. Your deepest wound could become your most powerful weapon against the enemy's lies. Your hardest trial could become your most effective tool for helping others.

But none of that can happen if you keep your wounds hidden. God can't use what you won't acknowledge. He can't heal what you won't reveal. He can't transform what you won't surrender.

Healing Requires Honesty

You don't heal by pretending it didn't hurt. You don't heal by avoiding it.

You heal by being honest, with God and with yourself.

Tell Him: "God, I'm tired." "I still hurt from what they did." "I don't know how to forgive." "I don't know how to trust again."

And watch what happens when honesty meets His hands.

Honesty is the first step in any healing process.

You can't treat a wound you won't acknowledge. You can't heal from trauma you refuse to admit. You can't recover from pain you pretend doesn't exist.

Honesty is difficult for men because we've been taught that admitting pain is admitting weakness.

We've been conditioned to believe that acknowledging wounds is a sign of defeat.

We've been programmed to think that talking about hurt makes us sound like victims.

But that's not biblical thinking, it's cultural programming that contradicts God's design for healing.

Throughout Scripture, we see men being honest about their pain, their struggles, their failures, and their desperate need for God's intervention.

David was honest about his pain when he wrote Psalms expressing abandonment, betrayal, and overwhelming sorrow.

Job was honest about his suffering when he questioned God amid unimaginable loss.

Jeremiah was honest about his discouragement when he became known as the weeping prophet.

Jesus was honest about His anguish when He sweat drops of blood in the Garden of Gethsemane.

Honesty doesn't make you weak, it makes you real. Vulnerability doesn't make you less of a man, it makes you more human.

Admitting your need for healing doesn't disqualify you from leadership, it qualifies you for authentic influence.

When you're honest with God about your pain, you create space for Him to work.

When you acknowledge your wounds, you invite Him to heal them.

When you admit your brokenness, you position yourself to receive His restoration.

How to Start Living This Scripture Daily

Stop Minimizing Your Pain Don't compare your wound to someone else's. If it hurts you, it matters to God.

Every man tends to minimize his own pain by comparing it to others:

- "At least I didn't have it as bad as..."
- "Other people have been through worse..."
- "I shouldn't complain because..."

But pain isn't a competition. Wounds don't need to be ranked to be real. Trauma doesn't have to be extreme to be valid. If it hurt you, it matters. If it affected you, it's significant. If it's still shaping your life, it needs to be addressed.

God doesn't operate with a hierarchy of pain. He doesn't heal only the deepest wounds while ignoring the smaller ones. He doesn't prioritize certain traumas over others.

Every wound matters to Him, because every person matters to Him.

Make Space to Be Still

Turn down the noise. Create space for God to speak, sometimes, healing begins in silence.

Many men stay busy to avoid confronting their pain. They pack their schedules with work, activities, and distractions to keep from sitting still long enough for their wounds to surface.

But healing requires stillness. It calls for quiet moments where you're not performing, producing, or protecting. It demands space where you can finally feel what you've been avoiding, acknowledge what you've been denying, and process what you've been postponing.

Making space to be still doesn't mean being inactive—it means being intentional. It means carving out time for reflection, prayer, and honest self-examination. It means creating environments where God can speak without having to compete with the noise of your busy life.

Invite Him Into the Specific Wound

Don't just pray, "Lord, heal me." Say, "God, I'm broken in this area, help me forgive my father, release that betrayal, and let go of that shame."

General prayers produce general results. Specific prayers invite specific healing.

God wants to heal your precise wounds, not just your overall brokenness. He desires to address the exact pain that's been affecting your relationships, your self-image, your ability to trust, and your capacity to love.

Inviting God into specific wounds requires you to identify and name your pain. It means getting honest about what happened, how it impacted you, and where you truly need healing. It means shifting from vague acknowledgment to raw, detailed honesty.

Trust That He Can Restore What Feels Too Far Gone

No wound is too deep. No scar is too ugly. God is not afraid of your brokenness, He's drawn to it.

The enemy wants you to believe that some wounds are too severe to heal, some pain too deep to restore, and some brokenness too complete to repair.

But that's a lie. There is no wound too deep for God's healing touch. No pain too great for His restorative power. No brokenness too complete for His redemptive love.

God specializes in impossible cases. He takes what seems irreparable and makes it better than it was before. He transforms scars into testimonies, wounds into wisdom, and pain into purpose.

Trusting God with what feels too far gone requires faith, faith that His power is greater than your pain, His love is stronger than your wounds, and His grace is sufficient for your healing.

The Journey of Healing

Healing is a journey, not a destination. It's a process, not a one-time event. It unfolds over time through consistent surrender, honest acknowledgment, and patient trust in God's restorative work.

This journey includes seasons of progress and seasons of setback, moments of breakthrough and moments of struggle, times when healing feels swift and times when it feels painfully slow. But every step of the journey matters. Every moment of honesty contributes to healing. Every act of surrender creates space for restoration.

It also involves discovering that your wounds, once healed, can become sources of strength instead of sources of shame. Your scars become testimonies of God's faithfulness. Your pain becomes a platform to help others. Your brokenness becomes a bridge to reach those who need to know that healing is possible.

Living as a Healed Man

When you let God heal what you won't talk about, you don't just feel better, you become better.

You don't just recover from your wounds, you're transformed through the healing process.

You don't just move past your pain, you become equipped to help others move through theirs.

Healed men love differently because they're no longer protecting wounds.

They lead differently because they're not compensating for pain.

They father differently because they're not passing down trauma.

They live differently because they're no longer managed by unhealed hurts.

Healed men also understand that healing is a continual process.

They don't pretend to be perfect or completely whole.

They continue to invite God into new areas of brokenness as He reveals them.

They remain open to His surgical work because they've experienced the freedom that divine healing brings.

Closing Declaration

"I no longer hide my wounds; I hand them to the Healer. I release the pain I've carried in silence. I am no longer just surviving, I am healing. Piece by piece. Prayer by prayer. Day by day."

Brother, it's time to stop bleeding in silence. It's time to stop pretending the wounds don't exist.

It's time to stop carrying pain that was meant to be healed. God sees every hurt you've hidden, every wound you've covered, and every pain you've buried.

He's not shocked by your brokenness, He's moved by it. He's not repulsed by your wounds, He's drawn to them. He's not impatient with your healing, He's invested in it.

You don't have to carry this alone anymore. You don't have to pretend you're fine when you're not. You don't have to hide your wounds to protect your image.

You have a God who heals the brokenhearted and binds up their wounds.

Let Him heal what you're afraid to talk about. Let Him bind what you've been hiding. Let Him restore what life tried to steal. Your healing isn't just about you, It's about every life you'll touch once you're whole.

Prayer

Father, I confess that I've been hiding wounds that need, Your healing touch. I've been carrying pain that I was never meant to bear alone.

I've been pretending, I'm fine when I'm broken, acting strong when, I'm weak, smiling when, I'm bleeding.

I've been hiding every pain, I've been carrying, every scar I've been covering.

Heal my broken heart. Bind up my wounds. Restore what life tried to steal. Your healing process. Make me whole so I can help others find wholeness.

In Jesus' name,

Amen.

William "King" Hollis

Reflection Questions

- What wound am I still hiding from others and even from myself?
- Have I invited God into the specific area of my life that still hurts?
- What lies have I believed about my pain that keep me from healing?
- How would my life look different if I truly let God bind and heal what's broken in me?
- What would it mean for my family, my relationships, and my purpose if I experienced complete healing in my deepest wounds?

CHAPTER 11: Let Love Kill the Fear

"There is no fear in love. But perfect love drives out fear."

– 1 John 4:18

Introduction: Fear Will Talk You Out of What Love Was Trying to Give You

Fear has stopped many men from trusting again, opening themselves to love, admitting they're hurting, and allowing someone to see their truth.

Because fear whispers: "If they really knew you, they'd leave." "Don't get too close, remember what happened last time?" "You can't show weakness. Stay guarded."

But 1 John 4:18 flips the script: "There is no fear in love. But perfect love drives out fear."

That means the answer to fear isn't more control. It's not about being colder, tougher, or more "unbothered." The answer is love.

This Scripture addresses a deep root that holds many men back from healing, vulnerability, and genuine connection: fear.

Fear of being hurt, judged, abandoned, or misunderstood. But it doesn't just say "don't be afraid", it shows us what actually kills fear: love. Not fake love. Not manipulative love. But perfect love, God's kind of love.

Fear is one of the enemy's most effective weapons against men because it disguises itself as wisdom, protection, and strength.

Fear tells you that staying guarded is smart. Fear convinces you that emotional walls are signs of maturity.

Fear whispers that vulnerability is weakness, and opening your heart is an invitation to pain.

But fear is a liar.

Fear doesn't protect you from pain, it prevents you from healing.

Fear doesn't keep you safe, it keeps you stuck. Fear doesn't make you strong, it makes you small. Fear doesn't preserve your heart, it imprisons it.

Why Fear Has Been Lying to You

Fear always makes you focus on the worst-case scenario. Love helps you focus on the greater good.

Fear says, "Protect yourself." Love says, "Surrender to what heals you."

Fear keeps you locked in survival mode. Love calls you into healing mode.

God's love doesn't just comfort you, it confronts the fear that has ruled your life for far too long.

Fear operates from a place of scarcity, believing that love is limited, that trust is dangerous, and that vulnerability always leads to pain. But that's not the truth about love, that's the lie wounded hearts believe.

Fear is rooted in past pain. Every time you've been hurt, betrayed, abandoned, or rejected, fear takes notes. It builds a case against vulnerability, gathers evidence against trust, and constructs arguments against ever opening your heart again. Fear becomes your self-appointed attorney, defending the reasons why you should never risk being hurt again.

But fear's counsel is always based on past evidence, not present possibilities. It judges today's opportunities by yesterday's pain. It assumes that what happened before will happen again. Fear believes all people are like those who hurt you, that every situation will end like the ones that broke you.

Fear also masquerades as wisdom. It tells you that caution is maturity, that keeping your guard up is being smart, and that expecting the worst is being realistic. But fear isn't wisdom, it's wounds that haven't healed. Fear isn't protection, it's prison bars disguised as security.

The most dangerous lie fear tells is that you're safer alone than you are loved.

Fear convinces you that isolation is better than intimacy, that loneliness is safer than vulnerability, that being guarded is wiser than being open. But that's not safety, it's slavery to past pain.

What is "Perfect Love"

It's not people-pleasing. It's not performance-based love. It's not "I love you when you do what I want."

Perfect love is unconditional, unshakable, unbreakable, and rooted in Christ.

God's love says:
- "Even at your worst, I never left."
- "Even when you failed, I still called you Mine."
- "You don't have to earn this, just receive it."

And when you live from that love, fear loses its grip. Perfect love is fundamentally different from human love.

Human love is often conditional, it depends on performance, reciprocity, and compatibility.

It can be withdrawn when you disappoint, diminished when you fail, and destroyed when trust is broken.

But God's love doesn't operate by human rules. His love isn't based on your performance.

His affection isn't weakened by your failures. His commitment to you isn't conditional on your faithfulness to Him.

His love is perfect, not because it never faces disappointment, but because it never gives up despite it.

Perfect love doesn't mean God overlooks your sin or ignores your failures.

It means He loves you in spite of your sin and through your failures.

It doesn't mean God doesn't care about your choices, it means His love for you isn't determined by them.

When you understand perfect love, it transforms how you see yourself.

You stop defining yourself by your worst moments and start identifying yourself by God's unchanging love.

You stop seeing yourself as damaged goods and start seeing yourself as a treasured child.

You stop believing you're too broken to be loved and begin to understand that God's love is what makes broken things beautiful.

Perfect love also transforms how you relate to others.

When you're secure in God's perfect love, you don't look to others to fill the void only He can fill.

You don't enter relationships from a place of neediness, but from a place of wholeness.

You don't love others to get something, you love to give something.

Why You Must Implement This Scripture

If you don't, you'll keep sabotaging healthy relationships, hiding from your calling because you're afraid to fail, numbing pain instead of facing it with love, and building walls instead of bridges.

You'll mistake distance for strength, when it's really just fear in disguise.

Love isn't weakness, it's warfare. It's how God defeats the fear that keeps whispering, "You're not enough."

Implementing this Scripture isn't just about feeling better, it's about living better.

It's about making decisions rooted in love instead of fear, approaching relationships with trust instead of suspicion, and pursuing purpose with confidence instead of anxiety.

When you don't apply this truth, fear becomes your counselor, your protector, and your guide. It influences every decision you make, every relationship you enter, and every opportunity you consider.

Fear keeps you small when God created you for greatness. Fear keeps you hidden when God called you to influence. Fear keeps you isolated when God designed you for community. Fear also steals the very things it claims to protect.

In trying to avoid pain, fear blocks your access to joy. In trying to avoid rejection, it keeps you from receiving love. In trying to avoid failure, it stops you from pursuing success.

But when you apply this Scripture, when you let perfect love drive out fear, you begin to live from a different place.

You start making decisions based on faith instead of fear, love instead of self-protection, and hope instead of past pain.

You begin taking risks that may lead to blessing, instead of avoiding risks out of fear of disappointment.

Living this truth means refusing to let fear have the final word in your relationships, your calling, your ministry, and your dreams.

It means recognizing fear's voice, and choosing to listen to love's voice instead.

It means identifying when you're operating from fear, and consciously choosing to operate from love.

How Perfect Love Drives Out Fear Practically

Love Tells You You're Safe in God, No matter what others do or say, God's love is your anchor. You are not abandoned, you are anchored.

When you're rooted in God's perfect love, other people's behavior no longer determines your security. Their acceptance doesn't define your worth. Their rejection doesn't diminish your value.

This doesn't mean you become reckless or naïve in relationships. It means you approach them from a place of security, not insecurity. You engage with others from strength, not from need. You love without the fear that their response defines your identity.

Love Makes You Honest

You stop pretending. You start healing. You're finally able to say, "This is who I am, and I'm still loved."

Perfect love creates an environment where honesty feels safe, vulnerability is welcomed, and authenticity is valued above image management.

When you know you're perfectly loved, you no longer feel the need to maintain perfect performance.

You can admit your struggles without fearing rejection. You can confess your failures without fearing abandonment. You can reveal your wounds without fearing judgment.

Love Sets You Free to Be Vulnerable

Vulnerability becomes a strength, not a risk, when you know you're already accepted by God.

When you're secure in perfect love, vulnerability isn't dangerous, it's powerful. It becomes a bridge to deeper relationships, not a threat to your safety.

Vulnerability stops being about the risk of rejection and starts being about the opportunity for connection.

It stops being about what you might lose and starts being about what you might gain.

It stops being a sign of weakness and starts becoming a mark of strength.

Love Gives You Power Over Shame

Where love is present, shame cannot survive. God's love covers what fear tried to expose in order to humiliate you.

Shame thrives in darkness, secrecy, and isolation, but love brings light, openness, and connection.

When perfect love shines on shame, shame loses its power.

Perfect love doesn't deny the reality of your failures, it redefines their significance.

Your mistakes don't define you when you're defined by God's love.

Your past doesn't determine your future when you're embraced by everlasting love.

The Battle Between Love and Fear

In every situation, you face a choice: love or fear. Every decision is influenced by one or the other. Every response is driven by love or fear. Every relationship is approached through the lens of love or fear.

Fear tells you to protect yourself at all costs. Love invites you to open yourself to possibility.

Fear warns you of what could go wrong. Love reminds you of what could go right.

Fear clings to past pain. Love leans into future potential. This battle isn't just philosophical, it's deeply practical.

When someone hurts you, do you respond with love or fear?

When you're presented with a new opportunity, do you step forward in love or retreat in fear?

When vulnerability is required in a relationship, do you choose to risk love or retreat to fear?

The battle is ongoing because fear rarely gives up easily.

Fear has been your companion for years, maybe decades. It knows your weaknesses, your triggers, your wounds. And it will continue to offer its counsel, its protection, its perspective.

But as you grow in understanding God's perfect love, the voice of love becomes louder than the voice of fear. Love's truth becomes more persuasive than fear's lies. Love's promises become more powerful than fear's warnings.

How to Start Living This Scripture Out

Soak in God's Love Daily, Speak it out loud: "I am fully loved by God, and there is no fear in His love." Let that be your truth, especially when fear tries to take hold.

This isn't positive thinking, it's a declaration of truth. You're not trying to convince yourself of something that isn't real. You're reminding yourself of what is real, but often forgotten.

Soaking daily in God's love means meditating regularly on Scriptures that reveal His heart toward you. It means spending time in prayer, not just asking for things, but receiving His love. It means starting each day grounded in the truth that you are beloved, not because of what you'll do that day, but because of who you are in Christ.

Let God's Love Redefine What You Deserve

You are not defined by your mistakes or your past. You deserve healthy love because God has declared you worthy. Fear tells you that your past disqualifies you from future blessings. Fear whispers that your mistakes make you unworthy of good things. Fear argues that your failures prove you don't deserve love.

But God's love redefines your worth. His love declares that you are valuable, not because of what you've done, but because of who He is. His love proclaims that you are worthy, not because you've earned it, but because He has chosen you.

Stop Letting Fear Lead Your Decisions

Ask yourself: "Is this choice coming from love or fear?"

Let love, not fear, be the compass that guides your relationships, goals, and healing.

This kind of discernment requires developing awareness of your motivations. Before making major decisions, pause and examine your heart. Are you choosing this because love is leading you toward growth, healing, and connection? Or are you choosing it because fear is pushing you toward safety, control, and self-protection?

Fear-based decisions may feel safer in the moment but often lead to regret. Love-based decisions may feel riskier at first, but they tend to lead to lasting growth.

Choose to Love Others Bravely

Loving others through hurt, rejection, and misunderstanding isn't easy, but it's how you become fearless.

When you choose to love despite the risk of being wounded, you declare that love is stronger than fear in your life.

Brave love doesn't mean being naive or ignoring red flags. It means approaching relationships with hope instead of suspicion, with trust instead of cynicism, and with openness instead of walls.

Brave love also means loving people who don't love you back, forgiving those who hurt you, and believing in people even when they let you down.

This isn't weakness, it's the strongest thing you can do.

Living Fearlessly in a Fearful World

When you let perfect love cast out fear, you become a different kind of man in a world full of fearful men.

You become someone who takes risks for the right reasons, who loves without guarantees, who hopes in spite of disappointment. You become a man who doesn't let past pain define present possibilities. You become someone who refuses to let the fear of rejection keep you from pursuing connection. You become a person who doesn't let the possibility of failure stop you from striving for success.

Living fearlessly doesn't mean being reckless. It means being so deeply rooted in perfect love that fear loses its power to control your decisions. It means being so secure in God's love that you're willing to risk being hurt by others.

It means being so confident in your identity in Christ that you can withstand rejection from people.

Fearless living also means becoming a safe place for those still held captive by fear. When fear no longer drives you, you're free to extend the same unconditional love that once freed you. You become a living demonstration of what perfect love looks like in human form.

The Transformation That Comes From Perfect Love

When perfect love drives out fear, it doesn't just change how you feel, it changes how you live.

You approach relationships differently. You make decisions differently. You face challenges differently. You see yourself differently.

You stop living defensively and start living with intention. You stop shielding yourself from life and begin engaging with it. You stop avoiding pain and start pursuing purpose. You stop being driven by what you're running from and begin being led by what you're running toward.

Perfect love also transforms your ability to love others. When you're no longer afraid of being hurt, you can love more freely. When you're no longer focused on self-protection, you can focus on serving others. When you're secure in God's love, you're able to give love rather than grasp for it.

Closing Declaration

"God's perfect love lives in me. I am not ruled by fear. I am loved, chosen, and safe. I will walk boldly, love deeply, and heal completely.

Love is not my weaknessit's my weapon." Brother, fear has held you captive long enough.

It has talked you out of opportunities, relationships, dreams, and healing.

It has convinced you that staying small is staying safe, that being guarded is being wise, and that avoiding love means avoiding pain.

But you don't have to be ruled by fear anymore. You don't have to make decisions based on worst-case scenarios.

You don't have to approach relationships with your walls up and your heart closed.

Perfect love has come to set you free. Perfect love has come to drive out fear. Let love silence the fear. Let perfect love drive out every lie fear ever told you.

About yourself., About others., About God., About life. Let love lead you.

You were created to love and to be loved. You were designed for connection, not isolation. You were called to live boldly, not fearfully. Perfect love makes all of this possible.

Prayer

Father, I confess that fear has been ruling too many areas of my life.

I've been making decisions based on fear instead of faith, Approaching relationships with suspicion instead of hope, I receive Your perfect love today.

I believe that Your love for me is unconditional, unshakeable, and unbreakable.

Let Your perfect love drive out every fear that has been holding me back.

Help me to love others bravely, to pursue purpose boldly, and to live fearlessly because

I'm anchored in Your love. Transform my heart from a place of fear to a place of love. Make me a demonstration of what perfect love looks like.

In Jesus' name,

Amen.

William "King" Hollis

Reflection Questions

- Where has fear been holding me back from giving or receiving love?
- What lies has fear been telling me about myself or my relationships?
- How would I show up differently if I truly believed I was fully loved and fully safe in Christ?
- Who do I need to love more bravely without fear, pride, or hesitation?
- What decisions am I making from fear that I need to remake from love?

Conclusion: Love Them More Than Your Demons

If You Only Remember One Thing If you've made it to the end of this book, it means you've walked through pain, truth, and some chapters that cut deep.

You've faced the boy in you who was never healed... You've confronted the man in you who's been hiding behind survival...

And you've been reminded of the God within you who's been fighting for your freedom all along.

But if you forget every Scripture, if you can't recall a single chapter title, if all the reflection questions blur together, remember this one truth:

- You are still worth loving, even with your wounds.
- Your pain does not disqualify you.
- Your past doesn't cancel you.
- Your demons don't define you.

God saw it all, and still chose you, still calls you, still covers you. This journey isn't about being perfect, It's about being real enough to let God work on the parts you've hidden, even from yourself.

So if you remember anything, remember this:

Healing is possible. Love is stronger than pain. God still wants you, not just the polished version, not just the version people applaud, but you, the real you.

You can love them beyond their demons. And it starts with loving yourself.

What It Means to Love More Than Your Demons

To love someone more than their demons doesn't mean ignoring their darkness, it means seeing it… and still choosing to stand with them in the light.

It's not weakness. It's not enabling. It's not pretending the hurt didn't happen.

It's choosing compassion over control, faith over fear, and grace over judgment, because that's exactly what God chose for you. He saw your demons, and still called you chosen. He saw your mess, and still declared you worth dying for.

To love someone more than their demons means:
- You don't confuse brokenness with worthlessness

- You understand that healing is a process, not a performance
- You give space for growth, not just demand perfection
- You hold up a mirror to the truth, but you never throw it like a weapon

It means staying when the world walks away, not always physically, but spiritually. You keep praying. You keep believing. You love them enough to hold them accountable, and enough to never give up on their potential.

But make no mistake: loving someone more than their demons doesn't mean losing yourself in the process. It doesn't mean excusing abuse or sacrificing your peace. It means learning to love with wisdom, to fight through intercession, and to walk in the kind of radical forgiveness that sets both of you free.

This love isn't natural, it's supernatural. It's the kind of love that says:

"I see the demon, but I also see the destiny. I hear the anger, but I also hear the ache. I feel the tension, but I also feel the tenderness still buried beneath. I won't worship your wounds, but I won't abandon you because of them, either."

The Power of Supernatural Love

To love them more than their demons is to say:

"You are not what hurt you. You are not what you've done. And I believe in who you can become, because I remember who God was for me when I was lost too."

This kind of love isn't soft, it's warfare. But if we truly want to see healing in our families, communities, and relationships, this is the kind of love that changes generations.

When you love someone more than their demons, you're partnering with God in spiritual warfare. You're refusing to let the enemy use their pain to define their identity. You're standing in the gap when they don't have the strength to stand for themselves. You're speaking life when all they can hear is death.

This kind of love requires supernatural strength because it defies every human instinct for self-preservation. It requires divine wisdom to discern the difference between helping and enabling. And it requires spiritual insight to love the person while resisting the demons that oppress them.

But this is exactly the kind of love that transforms lives. It's the kind of love that breaks generational curses.

The kind that turns prodigals into preachers, addicts into advocates, and wounded warriors into healers of others.

Love Like God Loves

So, what does it mean to love them more than their demons?

It means you love like God, no conditions, no contracts, just covenant.

You don't just love the version of someone that's easy, you love the version that needs grace the most.

And that kind of love?, That's the love that breaks chains. That's the love that turns addicts into fathers. That's the love that turns prodigals into preachers. That's the love that turns pain into purpose. That kind of love... is how we win.

God's love doesn't wait for you to get your act together before it shows up. It doesn't require perfection before it covers you. It doesn't demand that you eliminate all your struggles before it embraces you. God's love meets you in your mess, and transforms you in your brokenness.

When you love like God does, you become a reflection of His heart for the broken.

You become a safe place for people to bring their wounds. You become a source of hope for those who've given up on themselves.

You become living proof that change is possible, that healing is real, and that love truly can conquer all.

The Journey Continues

This book isn't the end of your journey, it's the beginning. Every chapter you've read, every truth you've uncovered, every wound you've acknowledged, all of it has been preparation for the life God longs to give you. It's all equipping you to love others the way He has loved you.

You've learned that the battle within is real, but victory is possible. You've discovered that weakness can become a weapon when surrendered to God. You've come to understand that loving through the storm is what makes love powerful. You've realized that condemnation has no place in the life of a believer.

You've seen that fatherlessness doesn't disqualify you from sonship. You've learned that healing requires effort, not just desire. You've recognized that control is an illusion, but trust is a choice. You've discovered that survival is possible, but thriving is the goal.

You've been reminded that healing happens in community, not in isolation. You've learned that hidden wounds produce hidden dysfunction. You've understood that perfect love drives out fear. And you've been equipped to love others more than their demons.

Your Assignment

Now comes your assignment: take what you've learned and live it. Take the healing you've received and share it. Take the love you've experienced and give it. Take the freedom you've found and help others find it too.

Your pain wasn't pointless, it was preparation. Your struggle wasn't meaningless, it was training. Your wounds weren't just wounds, they were qualifications for ministry.

God doesn't waste anything, especially pain. He uses it all for His glory and for the good of others.

You have a story to tell now, not just of brokenness, but of healing. Not just of struggle, but of victory. Not just of demons, but of deliverance.

Your story has the power to give hope to someone who feels hopeless, to encourage someone who's ready to give up, to inspire someone to keep fighting.

But your assignment isn't just to tell your story, it's to live it. It's to become the man God always intended you to be. It's to love with the same love you've received. It's to extend the same grace that was extended to you. It's to fight for others the way God fought for you.

The Ripple Effect

When you choose to love someone more than their demons, you're not just impacting one relationship, you're creating a ripple effect that reaches far beyond what you can see.

You're modeling to your children what healthy love truly looks like. You're showing your community what grace in action resembles. You're demonstrating to the world what God's heart looks like in human form.

Every person you love back to life becomes someone capable of loving others back to life. Every soul you refuse to give up on becomes someone who won't give up on others. Every demon you help someone conquer empowers them to help others conquer their own.

This is how transformation spreads. This is how healing multiplies. This is how love wins: one person at a time, one relationship at a time, one choice at a time, one act of supernatural love at a time.

Your decision to love someone beyond their demons could be the turning point in their story.

Your refusal to give up on them might be what keeps them from giving up on themselves.

Your commitment to see their potential, not just their problems, could be what helps them see it too.

Final Charge

Brother, you have everything you need to love them beyond their demons.

You have God's love flowing through you. You have His strength sustaining you. You have His wisdom guiding you.

You have His grace covering you. You don't have to be perfect to love perfectly. You don't have to be fully healed to help others heal.

You don't have to have all the answers to point others to the Answer.

You just have to be willing to love as you've been loved. The world is full of people battling demons they can't name, carrying pain they can't express, and fighting wars no one else can see.

They need someone who will love them beyond their demons. They need someone who sees their potential, not just their problems.

They need someone who believes in their destiny instead of defining them by their history.

That someone could be you. Will you accept the assignment?

Will you choose to love supernaturally? Will you commit to seeing people through God's eyes rather than through human judgment? Will you dare to love them beyond their demons?

The choice is yours. The power is available. The love is unlimited.

The only question left is this:

Will you step into your calling to love the way God loves? Your healing journey isn't complete until it becomes someone else's hope.

Your freedom isn't fulfilled until it becomes someone else's path to freedom.

Love Them More Than Your Demons

Your love isn't perfected until you give it to someone who doesn't deserve it, just like you didn't deserve the love that saved you.

Love them more than their demons. Start with yourself. Start today. Start now.

Final Prayer

To every man who picked up this book, whether you read every page or just one... whether you underlined every scripture or just fought through the tears this prayer is for you.

Father, I thank You for every soul who dared to open this book. For every man who's walked through trauma, been buried in silence, or worn strength as a mask just to survive another day.

God, I ask that You meet him right where he is in the middle of the mess, in the weight of the questions, in the shadows of the demons he's been fighting silently for years.

Wrap him in Your grace. Show him he is still worthy. Still redeemable. Still called. Still loved.

I pray that he no longer walks in shame but in freedom. Not in isolation but in truth. Not in bitterness but in bold, unshakable love.

Heal the broken boy inside of him. Strengthen the man who's trying to rise. And remind him every single day that You, Lord, are not afraid of his wounds. You came for them.

I speak peace over his mind. I speak clarity over his purpose. I speak forgiveness over his past. And I speak restoration over every relationship the enemy tried to destroy.

Let this not just be a book, but a turning point. A holy interruption. A chapter of healing that rewrites the rest of his story.

Let him love others more than their demons—starting with himself.

When the pain tries to rise again remind him, God: He's not alone. He's not too far gone. And he was never fighting by himself.

In Jesus' mighty, healing, chain-breaking name, Amen.

"Your pain has a purpose."

"Your demons don't define you."

"Your story isn't over."

William "King" Hollis

About the Author

William "King" Hollis is a globally recognized motivational speaker, author, and coach who has inspired millions through his story, his voice, and his unshakable belief in purpose over circumstance.

From experiencing homelessness and hardship to becoming one of the most in-demand voices in personal development, William's journey is a testament to the power of resilience, faith, and relentless determination. His raw and powerful storytelling has made him a voice for the voiceless, connecting deeply with people across all walks of life, from inner-city youth to Fortune 500 executives.

William made history in 2019 as the first and only paid motivational speaker to take the stage at Milan Fashion Week, a groundbreaking moment that signaled his rise on the international stage. His ability to command a room, uplift spirits, and shift mindsets has led to viral speeches, standing ovations, and over 400 million views on YouTube.

His message isn't just motivational it's transformational. William speaks directly to the hearts of those battling doubt, fear, trauma, and identity, reminding them that their pain has a purpose and their story still matters.

Whether he's delivering keynote speeches to global corporations, inspiring student-athletes, or mentoring the next generation of leaders, William brings authenticity, fire, and deep compassion to every platform he's given.

He is the author of the best-selling book, The Best Gift Comes From the Bottom
, and continues to spread hope worldwide through his content, coaching, and community impact.

www.ingramcontent.com/pod-product-compliance
Lightning Source LLC
Chambersburg PA
CBHW070640160426
43194CB00009B/1524